THE COUNTRY HABIT

JOSEPHINE HAWORTH

THE COUNTRY HABIT

METHUEN LONDON

First published in Great Britain in 1987
by Methuen London Ltd
11 New Fetter Lane, London EC4P 4EE
Copyright © 1987 Josephine Haworth

British Library Cataloguing in Publication Data

Haworth, Josephine
The country habit: a year in the working life of the land.
1. Natural history — Great Britain
I. Title
508.   41QH137

ISBN 0–413–41230–X

Printed in Great Britain by
Butler & Tanner Ltd, Frome and London

CONTENTS

ACKNOWLEDGEMENTS

The author and publishers wish to thank the following
for permission to reproduce copyright material: Carcanet Press Limited,
for extracts from *Selected Poems* by Elizabeth Daryush, 1972; Faber and Faber
Limited, for an extract from *Moortown* by Ted Hughes, taken from 'Little Red
Twin'; William Heinemann Ltd, for extracts from *The Land* by Vita
Sackville-West; Martin Secker & Warburg Limited, for
an extract taken from *The Complete Poetical Works
of Andrew Young*, Taken from 'Last Snow'.

The publishers are grateful to the following
for their kind permission to reproduce photographs in this volume:
the Beaford Archive – James Ravilious, for his frontispiece photograph
and for those at the beginning of February, March, April, June, July and November;
Landscape Only – P. Sutherland, for his photographs at the beginning of
January, September and December and for his tailpiece;
and Landscape Only – C. Waite, for his photographs
at the beginning of May, August and October.

INTRODUCTION

High on the fells of Cumbria, Harry Waller selects the next stone he needs for building a dry stone wall; Adam and Ben Pullen in Gloucestershire stop work on their farm for the pleasure of watching their cows go out for the first time in spring; Peter Philpot master-minds his farm managers in Essex by calling them up on his private radio system: 'Tiger. This is Tiger calling.'

These are just a very few pieces in the enormously varied and complex jigsaw that is our countryside. These people, and thousands like them, spend every waking hour, every day of the year, at work on the land. When we drive through the countryside we see the results of their efforts all around us, but to the untrained eye a field of corn or a flock of sheep or a herd of cows conveys very little.

The countryside can seem like a beautiful picture book, but the text, when we come to read it, is in a foreign language. To find out exactly what goes on in the farms and fields and forests as the seasons roll round, I talked not only to farmers and foresters, but to water bailiffs, gamekeepers and many others. It is the men with mud on their boots who can tell you what it is really like to shepherd a flock of sheep at lambing time or spend all day on a tractor ploughing a field furrow by furrow, or walk through the woods at night looking for poachers.

Everyone who travels through the countryside, even if it is only for a day's outing from the town, is aware of the changes that have altered the look of the land. Most crops are now sown in the autumn instead of the spring, grass is cut earlier and haystacks have disappeared, unfamiliar breeds of cattle graze in the fields; but most noticeable of all, while the fields and farms have grown bigger, the number of farm workers has declined. The day-to-day care of our land rests in the hands of an ever decreasing minority. Whereas in

1861 22 per cent of the working population of Britain were employed in agriculture, by 1961 it had dropped to 4 per cent and it is now well under 3 per cent. No wonder it is unusual to catch a glimpse of one of these rural survivors. The most the average country traveller is likely to see is a tractor to-ing and fro-ing across a field half a mile away. It would be nice to hop out of the car and talk to the tractor driver about the reasons behind all these changes. If you could only buttonhole the man he might also be able to tell you how the average farmer feels about the increasingly vocal criticism being levelled at the farming community. Twenty years ago farmers were seen on the whole as good old boys, battling against the elements to provide us with our food. Today they are regarded with suspicion, and accused of using their chemical sprays and high capacity machinery to produce unwanted surpluses and to damage the environment. So often the debate about conservation seems to be conducted by spokesmen and special interest groups: it makes a change to hear from a farmer how he regards conservation and how important the quality of his environment is to him. Even in an island as small as ours, the differences in climate, topography and temperature mean that there will be variations in the times that spring arrives or that the crops ripen. But nothing is regular. Nothing is certain. No two years are alike. In the right season any farmer, and particularly an arable farmer, will get on with the work he wants to do as soon as conditions permit, keeping a close eye on the sky rather than on the calendar. The country year has no beginning and no end. Something is growing all the time, whether it is crops maturing in the fields or young stock staggering into the world on uncertain legs. Planning and foresight are an important part of every farmer's way of life. 'A farmer should live as though he were going to die tomorrow,' the old saying goes, 'but he should farm as if he were going to live forever.' Even so, each month does have a meaning and personality of its own. Consequently, starting in January, I have followed the year through according to the calendar months and, from Cornwall to the Scottish borders and from East Anglia to West Wales, I have sought out the people at work, dogged their footsteps, asked them the sort of questions an interested spectator might want to ask and listened to what they had to say.

The result is not a treatise on the state of British agriculture today, but a series of passages to express the views of individuals. The variety of their lives and their experiences is extraordinary and yet they all make their own declaration of loyalty to their own part of the country in their own way. 'I'm not saying this is the best part of the country,' said one character. 'What I'm saying is, you'll not find a better.' Seen through the eyes of these people the conventional view of the countryside is transformed into something more real and more memorable. The images remain: Harry Waller selecting a stone and talking about the achievement of those men who first built the walls; Adam and Ben Pullen, the double-act from Gloucestershire; Venning Davey describing how he coaxed a herd of bullock across a stream in Cornwall; Tom Jones tending a sick calf in Wales; Leo Hiam laughing at the thought of a customs officer he frightened half to death with his lorry-load of live bees; Ivan Swaile standing on the moors of Northumbria, watching the curlew wheel and cry.

They may be only small pieces of the jigsaw but what they say helps to illuminate the whole picture. I am indebted to them all.

JANUARY

Our past is rooted in the countryside. Our forefathers lived there, worked there and belonged there. And yet, when we return to our lost paradise, the countryside often responds to our home-coming with a blank stare; a blur of green and brown as we drive past, a space between two places with no identity of its own.

Streets have names and so do fields, but the fields give nothing away. It might be Forty Acre Field you are looking at, or Poverty or Squire's Ground or Pig's Green or Bee Park or Mow Hay Meadow, but you would never know. It is the farmers and the foresters, the gamekeepers and the water keepers who have the inside story and, seen through their eyes, the countryside takes on meaning.

Even in unpromising January, when the woods are bare and *rigor mortis* seems to have set in in the fields, those who know the country best, like Emily Brontë, find something to celebrate:

> *The mute bird sitting on the stone,*
> *The dank moss dripping from the wall,*
> *The thorn-trees gaunt, the walls o'ergrown,*
> *I love them – how I love them all.*

To townspeople the winter comes as an uncomfortable, disconcerting and unnecessary ordeal, but in the country it has its purpose in the pattern of the year. The wind dries out the land, the frost breaks up the soil and the snow protects the grass from the worst of the cold. In his book *A Yeoman Farmer's Son*, H. Crump described his father:

> *Not so much a countryman as part of the country. For me, the wind and weather were constraints, for father they seemed a necessary and normal part of his working scene.*

I

When he worked outside in rain-sodden fields, he was the
rain and the earth, seeming to take the essence of them into
his person . . .

If the weather seems uncompromising, the farmers can match it
with a stubborn tenacity of their own. Farmers are patient people;
their philosophy goes back a long way. 'It's like it says in the Bible,'
one Cumbrian farmer explained simply: 'While the earth remaineth,
seed-time and harvest, and cold and heat and summer and winter
. . . shall not cease.'

In winter the shape and form of the landscape reassert themselves. Richard Jefferies, the nineteenth-century naturalist and
writer, said: 'Earth is always beautiful – always. Without colour, or
leaf, or sunshine . . . the power is ever there.' It is the time of year
when great flocks of birds sweep silently across the sky, and the
clean, long lines of the fields lead the eye away into the distance,
flying.

Down at ground level, the feeling of emptiness all around is partly
due to the fact that there are no cows to be seen in the fields.
Neither the black and white Friesians who make up the dairy herds
nor the mixed colours of the beef cattle. Not a single cow. It is not
so much that the cattle have to be taken inside for the winter because
they cannot stand the cold, but more to do with the fact that the wet
winter fields could not stand the trampling of the cows' feet. All
winter long the cows stay under cover and the men who look after
them have the job of cleaning them out and, if it is a dairy herd, of
milking them twice a day.

Ben and Adam Pullen on their farm in Churchdown, Gloucestershire, keep a dairy herd and their day starts at four-thirty in
the morning. 'It's dark at four-thirty on a January morning,' Ben
said, 'And bloody cold.'

The brothers share the work on the farm between them and take it in turns to get up to do the milking. Adam, the elder brother, is tall and dark and deliberate while Ben is sandy haired, quick-witted and decisive. The first job in the morning is to start up the milking parlour. 'We keep heaters going in the parlour in winter so that all those miles of pipes won't freeze up,' Ben said. 'The parlour's the warmest place to be by a long way.'

When the gate is opened the cows come in, twelve at a time, to be milked.

'They usually come in in roughly the same order,' Adam said. 'You have your boss cows and your indians, just like people. When you go out at four-thirty in the morning the cows are stood up by the gate, waiting for you.'

'No, they're not,' Ben said.

'Yes, they are.'

'Well, only about ten of them are,' Ben said.

They agreed that not all the cows were waiting by the gate when they started.

It takes about ten minutes to milk each cow. The Pullens' cows give about 7,000 litres of milk a year from each cow, or 80 bottles per day per cow from the best cows in the herd. Milking the whole herd takes two hours and after that it takes another half-hour to wash out the parlour. The cows are fed at eight o'clock in the morning. Immediately after milking they go back to their cubicles for a lie-down.

'They like a sleep after milking,' Adam said. 'Just like women, really. They like a sleep after . . . you know, don't they?'

The cows are milked for the second time in the day at three o'clock in the afternoon.

'At least it's light when you start the second milking,' Ben said.

One of the most important jobs in January is to keep the water supply to the cowsheds from freezing up because cows drink vast quantities of water.

'I should think one cow would drink about twenty gallons a day. Milk is 87 per cent water, you know,' Ben said. 'The old boys always used to say that it took six gallons of water to make one gallon of milk.'

The Pullens' cows start calving in the autumn but some cows will still be calving in January.

3

'If a cow calves late in year, then you can't get her into calf again until two months after the calf is born and so she's going to be late again the next year,' Ben said. 'Some of the best cows, giving vast amounts of milk, are working at a tremendous rate and that puts so much stress on their bodies that it is sometimes more difficult to get them into calf.'

The cows that have calved in autumn will be coming into season in January. A cow has a three-week cycle, so two months after calving – the next observed heat – is the time to call in either the bull or the artificial insemination man – in the Pullens' case, it is the artificial insemination man.

'Detection is the most important part of the job,' said Adam. 'You've got to know when she's ready.'

'We study the cows every day to watch for changes in their behaviour,' Ben said. 'Sometimes it's perfectly obvious because the cows start mounting each other, but with shy breeders you have to . . .' He looked around for inspiration. 'You have to use as much experience as you can lay your hands on,' he said carefully. 'Sometimes they come up and love you,' Adam explained, 'or they stand at the gate mooing.'

'You've got to know your cows pretty well,' Ben said.

The master plan for the Pullens' artificial insemination programme starts well before Christmas when the brochure of available bulls arrives through the post. The brochure is full of beautifully photographed bulls in full colour with details of their conformation (shape), the milk yield from cows bred from them, the temperament of their progeny and everything else a prospective customer might want to know.

'It is a Friesian bull we are looking for,' Ben said. 'A *British Friesian*,' he added firmly.

The Pullens place their order in good time and the 'straws' of semen are then stored, frozen, at the AI Centre. The 'straws' are like drinking straws but much thinner and about five inches long, and each contains a minute amount of semen. Ben likes to get his order in early because a really good bull could be so popular that there might be a waiting list, in which case, he explained, 'It's first come first served.' Then he realised what he had said and burst out laughing.

4

'That was rather well put, wasn't it?' he said, wiping his eyes while Adam roared and banged the table with approval.

Once the cows have been observed to be in season, Ben or Adam ring up the AI man, Mitch, and he will be at the farm by nine o'clock the next morning.

'Mitch comes every day from about November to January,' said Ben.

'No, he doesn't,' Adam said, 'not every day.'

'Well, nearly every day,' Ben said. 'And he AI's about seven or eight cows a day.'

The Pullens also keep a Hereford Bull on the farm to serve the heifers (young cows who will be calving for the first time) and 'to "mop up" round the cows when we have AI'd all we want to,' Ben said, adding that 'shy breeders will take to a bull more easily.' But of course the calves produced from the bull will be bred for beef because they will be Hereford/Friesian crosses, not dairy cows.

The Milk Marketing Board, which runs the Artificial Insemination Centre used by the Pullens, select the bulls which appear in their brochure very carefully. They buy a hundred young bulls every year and three to four hundred cows are inseminated from these bulls. The resulting calves are assessed and monitored at every stage of their development and it is seven years before the best bulls are finally chosen and get their picture in the colour pages. The best bull the Milk Marketing Board ever had was a Friesian called Grove Spectacular who fathered 300,000 calves during his lifetime and since the straws can be stored 'theoretically for ever', he is still siring calves now that he is dead.

Farmers pay £25 to £30 per straw for the best thirty or forty bulls on the books, but anyone who does not order in advance gets 'the bull of the day', which is whatever the Inseminator happens to have with him when he arrives. 'Taureau du jour' costs slightly less than a special à la carte order.

With careful planning and selective breeding, farmers can improve their herd with every new generation. Ben Pullen does not mind the hard work, being 'tied to a cow's tail' year-in and year-out.

'You never stop learning,' he said. 'Never.'

The fact that his milking cows produce more than average yields and that the premium beef cattle he takes to market sell for top prices and more often than not are declared 'Best of Market', pleases him enormously. Ben Pullen is quick and competitive; he is proud of what he and Adam are achieving with their herd.

While the dairy cows stay inside and produce a steady stream of milk and muck, most of the sheep are still out, backs to the wind, nibbling at the tired grass and being fed on hay and concentrates by their owners, because their lambs are growing inside them. Spring lambing sheep will be halfway through their pregnancy in January and in the next few weeks the weight of the embryo will increase from about half a pound to as much as ten pounds. In the South of England, however, early lambing has become a feature of sheep farming because early lambs are more profitable. The change cannot be brought about overnight because the ewes have to be brought into season earlier and earlier over a matter of years. One man I went to see in Cornwall had spent three years getting his first one hundred ewes ready to lamb in January. This was his first experiment with such early lambs and I was interested to see how it was turning out. Richard Willcox was looking cheerful when I saw him. Only twenty of the hundred ewes had lambed, but even so he was delighted with the way things were going. The ewes had been sheared before they lambed so that it would be easier to see exactly what condition they were in. It is unusual to see a slim-line sheep with a lamb and both of them equally clean and tidy. If you look at sheep out in the field, about the only thing you can tell for certain is whether they are standing up or lying down, or dead. The rest is wool.

Richard Willcox lambs the whole of his flock of 430 ewes indoors in a huge barn across the yard from the farmhouse, but the 100 early ewes were in a separate partition. We went and had a look at them and Richard Willcox explained that shearing the ewes had given rise to another, unexpected advantage.

'Without all that fleece,' he said, 'the lambs can find the teats so much more easily. They're the only thing they can grab hold of. I haven't had to put one single lamb on to suck so far and normally you spend an awful lot of time putting them on. I hadn't thought of that.'

Richard stood, leaning on the wooden barrier round the sheep pens.

'Imagine if this lot had been outside,' he said, 'I'd have lost half the buggers by now.'

Richard had put all the newly-born lambs and their mothers in the same pen for convenience, although it said in the textbooks that sheep with single lambs should be separated from sheep with twins.

'It seems to me that the twins are topping up their milk supply from the ewes with only one lamb. That, too, could be because the ewes have been sheared. All I can say for certain is that the ewes with singles are losing weight at the same rate as the doubles, so the milk must be going somewhere, mustn't it?'

The ewes had a constant supply of silage to eat and plenty of water to drink and on one side of the pen there was a wooden barrier with just enough room underneath for a lamb to get in. Inside this 'lambs creep', to the amazement of Richard Willcox himself and all the friends and neighbours who had popped in to see how things were going, there were a lot of lambs snoozing away comfortably between feeds, quite unconcerned about their mothers who were getting on with their breakfast/lunch/dinner outside. And, most surprising of all, there was not one worried bleat or baa to be heard anywhere.

Two pens down was the ante-natal ward where the sheep due to lamb were lying, cudding sleepily. A more smug-looking bunch of animals it would be hard to imagine. When a ewe starts to lamb, Richard explained, she decides on a place in the pen where she will give birth and keeps all the other ewes away.

'Wherever she is when the waters break, that's where she'll lamb,' he said.

The lambs born in January will be sold at between ten and fourteen weeks old and will be kept inside until then. Richard Willcox has been accused of factory farming and he doesn't like it.

'Where would you rather be in this weather?' he said. He gets very impatient with people who complain that early lambing deprives them of the pleasure of watching lambs frolicking in the fields in the spring. 'If it's a bad spring,' he said, 'you won't catch those same people bothering to go and stand out in the cold to watch the poor little buggers, will you?'

In the barn next door were all the rest of the ewes, due to lamb at the end of February. They were not shorn but, because they were being housed, they were surprisingly clean. Keeping his flock inside until they have lambed makes Richard's working life a lot easier. He can walk into the barn and see almost at a glance if everything is all right, whereas it would take him at least half an hour to walk round each field, checking on every sheep.

'If anything *is* wrong, it would take me a good deal longer than that,' he said. 'If a sheep is ill or in any kind of trouble, you can't catch the damn' things.'

One sheep, which looked identical to the rest, pushed its way out of the mass of cream coloured wool and came up to him.

'This is Daisy May,' he said, tickling her head. 'She was hand-reared and she's special. She'd follow me anywhere and where she goes the rest will follow. I'll keep her till she drops whether she produces any lambs or not.'

Sheep may not be the most intelligent of animals, but they do know what is good for them and in hard weather they like to be inside out of the cold and wet. Another romantic notion gone bust: those hardy, independent creatures of the wide open spaces are not such free spirits after all.

'My father would never have believed it,' Richard said. 'Not just my father, but a whole generation of sheep farmers genuinely believed that if you brought a sheep inside, it would die.' He laughed. 'Of course that might have had something to do with the fact that by the time they brought a sheep in, it would be half dead anyway.'

Lambing indoors is intensive sheep farming, while the hill farmers with their huge flocks and miles of upland grazing go in for extensive sheep farming.

'I was talking to a Welsh hill farmer on the telephone the other day,' Richard said. 'He was telling me that they had been snowed up for five days and nothing could get through. "What about the sheep?" I asked him. "Oh, they take care of themselves," he said.'

In fact they do not. Where possible the hill farmers bring their flocks down to be as near to the farmhouses as possible, but for some reason known only to God and sheep, a sheep will always walk with the wind and not against it, and when, eventually, it comes to a wall, it will take shelter there. Unfortunately, if it snows heavily, that is just where the drifts – driven by the wind – will pile up.

'She'll be on the wrong side of the wall,' said Richard. 'That's the trouble.'

According to Richard Willcox some hill farmers are lucky if they get one lamb from each ewe. With indoor lambing a ewe can rear two or even three lambs quite easily.

'They used to talk about something called "Twin Lamb Disease",' he said. 'There's no such thing. It's just that in harsh conditions the ewe hasn't the resources to rear two lambs.'

Although indoor lambing eliminates the problems of bad weather conditions, no flock can be entirely without its casualties. When Richard Willcox starts lambing in earnest at the end of February, about forty or fifty ewes will lamb in one day.

'There are lambs flying everywhere,' he said.

Inevitably there will be orphans. What happens then?

'We have a little trick,' Richard said.

Their little trick is to wait for a ewe to have a single lamb and if they think she has enough milk for two, they take an orphan, dip it in warm water, rub it all over with the afterbirth of the lamb that has just been born.

'And when it's all wet and steamy and slimy, we lie it down by the new mother,' he explained.

And will she accept it?

'There's a good chance that she will,' he said. 'And if she does we're giving the orphan the best chance we can. I don't like bottle-fed lambs. They never do so well, not even when they're weaned and turned out. Somehow they just don't seem to flourish in the same way as a lamb that has been mothered up.'

When all his ewes have lambed and the weather is right, Richard will turn his flock out into the fields.

'And they don't want to go,' he said. 'With cows and bullocks, once they know the grass is growing, they can't wait to get out, but the sheep would stay in here all year round if we let them. They don't even bother to look up and see what's going on outside. My father would never have believed it.'

On a very cold, bleak January day, when the wind was making storm at sea noises in the tops of the conifers and felt like knives at ground level, I was standing in a wood near Frant in Kent with John Hammond, Woodman/Warden for the National Trust. John Hammond was explaining that people are very 'tree conscious' these days. Too much so for his liking.

'They drive out and see a site where we've been doing some felling and they say we're destroying the countryside,' he said. His black moustache drooped unhappily.

As the man responsible for taking care of the woodlands and for creating an ideal habitat for the wildlife there, he is the last person who deserves to be criticised: the wood in which we were standing was due for some felling because he had decided to replace some of the conifers with broad leaved trees to give it more variety.

'What we are trying to do here is to set up a multi-layered structure of trees of different ages which will maintain a diversity of wildlife,' he says. He likes to talk in woodman-speak when he is wearing his official hat. 'This site is going to revert back to a more oak orientated structure,' he said. Right.

Good woodland management is not too neat.

'If you made everything too neat and tidy, you would have a nice tidy, empty wood,' John said. 'What we are trying to do is to speed up the evolutionary process to produce the right kind of habitat for all the birds, animals and insects we want to attract to the site. We normally plan ahead for about five years, but the vision has to extend to fifty or a hundred years.'

Having the vision to plant trees is a rare gift. John Hammond is not only concerned with restoring the woodlands under his control, but also has to replace some of the trees in the parks round the big houses owned by the National Trust.

'Some of the oak trees in the parkland must be five hundred years old,' he said. 'People seem to think they will last for ever, but they can't. You must have something growing up, ready to take their place one day. And that takes a lot of thought. The original trees were chosen and sited by the people who built the houses. You have to get a map and work out just where you are going to plant them. They are not just trees, they are key visual points in the landscape. To plant for the future far beyond your own lifetime takes a bit of faith I suppose.'

Centuries ago this far-sightedness was nothing out of the ordinary, but somehow the vision was lost. In the nineteenth century, Richard Jefferies was already regretting its passing:

> By old farmhouses . . . one or more huge walnut trees may
> be found. The provident folk of those days planted them
> with the purpose of having their own gunstocks cut out of the
> wood when the tree was thrown. . . . I like to think of those
> times, when men settled themselves down, and planted and
> planned and laid out their gardens and orchards and woods,
> as if they and their sons and sons' sons to the twentieth
> generation, were sure to enjoy the fruit of their labour.

Then the snow comes. Overnight every tree, every bush, every individual twig has flowered: dazzling white blossom is pillowed on the evergreens and outlined along the branches. Even the forgotten seedheads in the long grass balance their tottering snow hats with surprising grace. And while the frost lasts, there is a great and total silence over everything. The sheep out in the fields huddle humbly, numbed by the brightness all around them, belittled by its brilliance.

But the soft, gentle snow shows no kindness to the creatures whose world it has eclipsed. Birds fluffed out to twice their normal size against the cold move cautiously among the trees as if anxious not to bring down another avalanche from the branches around them. In the woods the search for food goes on in silent desperation. Only food can provide the warmth to sustain life and the tracks left from recent hunting expeditions are preserved in the snow to tell their own story; the criss-crossed morse code of rabbit tracks, two dots – two dashes, where forefeet and hind legs have rested, and the occasional bright orange splash where a buck rabbit has marked out his territory; the sharp arrow-shaped marks of the feet of pheasants, sometimes followed by a thin straight line where a cock pheasant has drawn his tail delicately over the surface of the snow; and deeper than all the rest, the tracks of a fox, each pawprint exactly in front of the last, a straight furrow leading from the trees and down the bank, purposeful and deliberate, a killer on the move.

As soon as the snow becomes a serious possibility, Andrew Jones, in West Wales, decides that it is time to bring his ewes down from the mountain. His mountain land is a thousand feet above sea level and four miles away from the main farm outside Lampeter. In that area of Wales many of the farms are family owned and the people, all Welsh speaking, are fiercely proud and protective of their heritage. Andrew Jones knows everyone in the district and everyone knows him. He works with one neighbour when he is making silage and another one when it is time to dip the sheep.

'It must be the last place in the country where farmers still actually get together and help one another. But on the whole I think that we are gradually becoming more independent,' he said, 'which is a pity really because I think in the past when people gathered together for the hay-making or the harvest it was a social occasion too, and I think that farming was probably more enjoyable because of that. Now it is all drive on, drive on.'

At thirty-two years old, Andrew Jones runs the farm practically single-handed although he is supported by a close-knit family of women. His young wife and children live in a cottage not far from the elegant white farmhouse occupied by his mother, aunt and sister. Since his father died ten years ago, Andrew has steadily been increasing the stock, putting up new farm buildings and improving some of the higher grazing ground with ploughing and reseeding.

'My father believed that you should never borrow money,' he said. 'But farming is different today. The tax man and I are good friends,' he said, laughing, 'I spend the lot.'

Andrew needs all his enthusiasm and restless energy to keep up with the changes in farm policy that have taken place in the last few years.

'Ten years ago, if you had a piece of land and didn't farm it, you were frowned on,' he said. 'Today if you do farm a piece of land you are frowned on.'

In 1981 he received a 50 per cent Government Grant for ploughing and reseeding one area of his 100 acres on the mountain, but today things are very different.

'I wouldn't get it,' he said. 'I wouldn't get anything if I applied now, and in a few years' time the conservationists might actually prevent me from improving the land. So I feel that everything I want to do, I've got to do *now*. It's something that is hanging over me all the time like Big Brother. I know conservation is here to stay – you used to be able to get grants to take out the hedges; now you can get grants for putting them back – but as long as the conservationists stay in the hedges I don't mind. If they ever stopped me farming, I'd really be up in arms.'

When Andrew decides it is time to bring the sheep down from the mountain, most of the family turn out to help. Mother, aunt and farm-workers all drive up to the mountain with the dogs and walk the sheep the four miles back to the farm. The ewes are Beulahs – hardy hill sheep – and the black-faced Llanwenogs. By the time Andrew and the family arrive to collect them they are ready to come, waiting patiently by the gate for the food Andrew has been bringing up for the past few weeks.

The scenery at a thousand feet is harshly beautiful. From the highest point of Andrew's land you can see right over to the Vans of Carmarthenshire and the Plynlimon Range.

'I remember coming up here one day on my own,' Andrew said. 'There was a heavy mist in the valleys but up here it was quite clear. I felt as if I was walking on the top of the clouds. I'll never forget that experience.

'This land up here will not have changed in five hundred years,' he went on. 'See all those heaps of stones we cleared when we were improving the grazing? The land here is covered with rocks like that. Farming in Wales can break you, you know. You see some of the old men round here: they're bent over, their hands are like shovels. They've worked so hard all their lives, they've worn themselves out.'

The family take one last look round the desolate beauty of the mountain before they leave it for the winter. As the sheep move downhill, guided by the family, Andrew calls his circling dogs to order – 'Jem, Jem, Jem, Jem. Nana, Nana, Nana, Nana. Derema (Come here). Gorwedd (Lie down).' From behind, the sheep look like a river of rounded woolly backs bouncing and hurrying over the pebbles, rushing downhill in an ever-moving stream.

Back in the farmhouse kitchen there is a hot midday meal for everyone: meat and vegetables, pudding and custard, tea and biscuits. The outside work done, the balance of power has shifted to the females of the family. Andrew tucks into second and third helpings of everything under the approving eye of his mother who gets up occasionally, smoothing down her flowered overall, and circulates with the teapot.

'Farming doesn't make economic sense any more,' he said, pausing for a moment. 'In the past I used to look forward to the time when the cows went out to grass and the milk yield would go up. I'd be looking in the milk tank every day, watching to see how much was there, and then the Milk Marketing Board lowered the price they paid for milk in the spring. It's like training racehorses and then being told it's not coming in first that counts, but the number of strides it takes or something like that. They've spoilt the spring for me now.

'Still, I've got the lambing to look forward to, haven't I?' he said. 'Farming is an addiction you know. Once it's in your blood, you become more and more involved until it takes up every waking hour of your life.'

FEBRUARY

February is a restless time of year. Winter is not yet over, but its welcome is wearing thin. The farmers are restless and so is the countryside: every living thing is looking for some sign of approaching spring. There is activity everywhere; small, individual bursts of energy responding to the least hint of warmth rather than one great orchestrated movement. Stray gusts of wind twirl a few dead leaves into a sudden spiral and tiny, tentative sounds and movements come from all directions. The birds have abandoned their winter flocks to fidget among the bushes, beginning to stake out their territorial claims before nesting starts in earnest. The tight, pointed buds on the twigs seem to twist and turn themselves towards the pale sun, reaching out towards the light. The sun can transform the cold world in an instant.

Richard Jefferies understood the effect of the early sun on human beings. In his book *Wild Life in a Southern Country* he wrote: 'We enjoy that peculiar genial feeling which is induced by sunshine at that period only, and which is somewhat akin to the sense of convalescence after a weary illness.' Exactly. The relief caused by a burst of sun may be short-lived, but there is a promise of softness in the air.

'You can stop believing that the weather is trying to kill you,' Charles Amos said.

Charles Amos, on his farm in Kent, suffers from 'sowing fever' in February like all arable farmers. Any crops not sown in autumn must be planted as soon as possible.

'If you hear the sound of a neighbour's tractor working in February, you are out of the house in a flash to see what he's doing; and then you have to try and decide whether he has jumped the gun or if the soil really is dry enough for planting,' he said.

In Gail Duff's book, *Country Wisdom*, there is some good advice about how to know when the soil is right for planting: 'If you can sit on the earth with your trousers down and it feels all right, sow your barley and it will be up in three days.'

'I use a soil thermometer myself,' Charles Amos said. 'You just stick it in the ground and look at it every morning.' The most important piece of advice offered about what to do at this stage is to go ahead as soon as possible, as we can see from an old guide to sowing in *Country Wisdom*.

> *Howe shall ye knowe the seasonable tyme?*
> *Go upon the lande, that is plowed and if it*
> *synge or crye, or make any noyse under*
> *thy fete, then it is to wet to soew:*
> *And if it will make no noyse and will bear thy*
> *horses, thanne sowe in the name of God.*

'Sowe in the name of God' is still as true today as it ever was.

'Never wait for tomorrow,' Charles said. 'If conditions are right, *use* them.'

It is not only the arable farmers who get restless in February; the stock farmers have their worries too. February 2nd, Candlemass, was traditionally the day on which 'A farmer should have half his corn and half his hay' still left to see his stock through the winter. The use of fertilisers has meant that farmers can now speed up the growth of spring grass but, even so, a lot of anxious glances are still cast over the remaining food stocks in February. Ben and Adam Pullen in Gloucestershire have a total of five hundred animals to feed through the winter. Does February ever give them the horrors?

'Never,' said Ben. 'We never ever run out before the spring. Never.'

'I suppose some people must do, though, mustn't they?' Adam said thoughtfully, trying to be fair. 'If they've had a poor summer and the weather stays too wet for them to get the cattle out until late on in the spring?'

'That's bad management, you twerp,' Ben said briskly.

Dick Bell can turn his hand to most things around the farm, but his passion is for shooting and especially pigeon shooting.

'If they push the nuclear button,' he said, 'I hope they do it while I'm out shooting pigeons and then I'll die happy.'

Pigeons are a problem at this time of year. When food is scarce they flock on to the kale planted by the farmers for their sheep, or they collect on the fields of oilseed rape. An official estimate puts the number of pigeons in this country at well over eight million birds; this number does not seem to vary greatly in spite of the fact that pigeon shooting is becoming more popular.

'People come out from the towns and bang away,' Dick Bell said, 'But I wouldn't say they did a lot of good.'

Dick had been pigeon shooting the previous day, and after four hours spent crouched in a hollow tree, his knees were still stiff.

'I didn't notice it while the birds were coming over,' he said, hobbling round in a circle, 'But when it was time to go home, I could hardly move.'

People who take pigeon shooting seriously – like Dick Bell – start at first light by studying the flight lines of the birds because pigeons keep to set flight-paths, and the first thing to do is to identify one of these. Then they get themselves somewhere directly underneath and well out of sight – pigeons have very sharp eye-sight.

Dick Bell leaned against the bonnet of his Land Rover and pulled a tobacco tin out of his pocket to roll himself a cigarette.

'Yes,' he said, 'I dropped thirty pigeons yesterday and I used about fifty cartridges. I didn't do too bad.'

The weather had been rough – perfect for pigeon shooting because bad weather forces the birds to fly at tree-top level. With the wind behind them, a flock of pigeons present a fast-moving target.

'Flighting with the wind, I would say they touch fifty or sixty miles an hour,' Dick said, 'but you always hope for a windy day to keep them down.'

One difficulty these days is that because more farmers are

growing oilseed rape, it gives the pigeons a choice of feeding grounds. If Dick finds that the flocks are splitting up, he uses decoys to bring the birds to him. Decoys are dummy pigeons, made out of rubber or metal and coloured with the distinctive wood-pigeon markings of two white bars on the upper wings and a white collar. Dick Bell opened the back of the Land Rover and moved some sacks to show me his decoys. They were kept under cover, he explained, because the local farmer did not approve of decoys.

'He thinks they attract more pigeons on to his crops,' Dick said. 'Silly really. What's the difference if you're going to shoot them anyway?'

When Dick is 'decoying' he sets up his hide with the wind behind him and puts the decoys on sticks on the ground so that they move slightly and look, from above, like real birds feeding. For some unaccountable reason, Dick explained that sometimes pigeons will respond to the decoys and that sometimes they will not. He asks no more than that sometimes they do. If they do, they will always come in with the wind and then sweep round and land against it.

'They spot the decoys from high up and if they are going to come in, they set their wings and come straight down,' he said. 'Sometimes they come in like bombs. It's hard to describe the feeling you get when you see them set their wings like that and you know they are coming for sure.'

Happiness for Dick Bell is a windy day, a gun in his hand and a flight of pigeons overhead. But once March comes and the pigeons start pairing off ready to breed, the shooting has to stop.

'You need a flock, you see,' Dick said. 'There's nothing doing then until about August when they start collecting on the fields again to feed on the seeds left behind by the combines.'

In the summer months Dick Bell does a bit of clay pigeon shooting. A clay pigeon is a disc propelled into the air mechanically for the guns to fire at.

'It's good sport,' Dick conceded, 'and it's quite a social occasion, but personally I prefer the real thing every time. There will never be anything to take its place.'

I suggested that at least clay pigeon shooting should keep the conservationists happy because nothing gets killed. Dick put away his battered old tobacco tin, lit up his cigarette and glanced at me with quiet amusement.

'Not necessarily,' he said. 'I went clay pigeon shooting in Norfolk once and one of the old boys was telling me that every time they went out shooting clays this old rabbit would come out and sit on the bank watching them. Then one day somebody missed a clay and it came down, thunk, on the rabbit's head, and that was the end of the rabbit. Shame, wasn't it?' he said, his smile spreading into a slow grin. 'They were quite upset.'

There is no pattern to a pig's year. They can breed in any season and since a sow's gestation period is three months three weeks and three days, breeding sows produce litters all year round.

Eddie Ireton is the tenant farmer of 200 acres high up on the fells above Hawkshead in the Lake District, where he keeps ninety-one suckler cows, two hundred and fifty breeding ewes and four hundred pigs for fattening. Four hundred pigs is not many by today's standards, but I had been told that what Eddie Ireton did not know about pigs was not worth knowing. It would be well worth the steep pull up from Hawkshead village to visit him, I was told, but unfortunately when I arrived at the low white farmhouse, Eddie Ireton was not at home. His family said he had gone to market with some cattle but that he was expected back shortly. In the meantime, his farmhand, Richard, invited me to go and see the pigs because he was just about to feed them. Eddie keeps the pigs in a huge shed behind the farm, separated into pens of forty by iron-barred partitions. I watched the pigs milling about while Richard went into the foodstore and filled up a wheelbarrow with a mixture of maize and rice, grassmeal and fishmeal, heaped into a golden mound in the barrow. As soon as Richard with his wheelbarrow appeared in the doorway to the shed there was an outbreak of noise from the pigs like several aircraft taking off in an echo chamber.

Richard grinned and, as he pushed his wheelbarrow into the wall of sound, I noticed that he was wearing ear-muffs.

'The Health and Safety people advise them,' he explained later. 'The noise is bad for your ears.'

Richard had brought Eddie Ireton's sheepdog with him and as he opened the partition to the second pen down he whistled to the dog, who hurried to the gap and stood head down, in a long mean line, threatening any pig who tried to come out. Once inside the pen, Richard wheeled his barrow into the middle and then stopped and began throwing food by the shovelful all over the pigs in the first three pens. As the food arrived, the sound stopped and there was just a rustling noise to be heard as the pigs ate. These were the oldest pigs and the noisiest ones. Richard took off his ear-muffs and in the silence we heard a car pulling up at the front of the farm.

'He's back,' Richard said.

The dog stared hard in the direction of the sound but didn't move: he had taken up position further down the shed and was up to his ankles in slurry.

'The dog's called Ben,' Richard said. 'DON'T SAY HIS NAME,' he added quickly, 'OR HE'LL JUMP UP ON YOU.'

The pigs are kept on restricted feeding to stop them getting too fat and are fed twice a day, getting about four pounds of food per pig per time. Quite apart from food, water is very important, so each pen has its own drinking trough with a constant supply of fresh water. The pens are scraped out with a hand-scraper every other day, but most of the dirt drains out into a channel in the centre of the building which leads into a slurry pit underground.

I had been staring at the pigs for some time before I realised what it was that was bothering me: instead of long, curly tails, they only had about two inches of tail, turning up like fat little apostrophes at the end of each pig. I went to look for Eddie Ireton and found him standing in the middle of the farmhouse kitchen with a face like stone. Eddie is a big man. He has, as they would say in the North of England, plenty of 'clout'. He explained that he had just had a terrible day at the market; he had brought the beasts back. That meant that two years of rearing and feeding them had gone for nothing.

'I wasn't happy with the price,' he said. 'Not at all. Sometimes you have to sell stock because you have to have the cash to buy in.'

In this case prices had been so low that he had withdrawn his animals from the sale and would try again in a couple of weeks when he *might* get a better price but he might not. The day had been a waste of time and money. Eddie had shown the animals himself.

'I think a man should be prepared to go and stand behind his stock,' he said. 'And, if you are in the ring with them, at least you are in the right place to put a stop to the sale if you don't like the price.'

The bad news was filtering through to everyone on the farm. Various members of the family came into the kitchen, took one look at Eddie's face and made themselves scarce.

Eddie took over the tenancy of this farm twenty-two years ago and at that time a great deal of the land was covered in bracken.

'The pigs used to run loose in the fields then,' he said, 'and we used to feed them pretty freely because people wanted big, fat pigs. We had five to six hundred pigs all running out in the fields. Pigs are bad to handle, you know. With a sheep you've the wool to grab hold of, but a pig – weighing something like 280 pounds – takes a bit of pulling about. Those we've got inside now; if one of those got out and you wanted to catch it, I reckon in half an hour it would be tired . . . but those we used to have outside, we had some fair old running-about sessions with those. With pigs, when you want to move them, you have to do it mostly by encouragement. Mostly you have to be nice to them, because the more you try to force them into doing something, the more they will rebel.'

Eddie talked quietly and easily, and when he had said all he had to say on a subject, he ended with a verbal full-stop – 'Mmmm'.

'The dog moves the pigs quite well – some dogs won't entertain pigs at all, you know,' he said. 'But then not all dogs get the chance to work with pigs, do they? Of course the dog is best with the sheep and he's not bad with the cattle either, except when the cows are out with their calves: that can be a problem because the calves chase the dog (just for a bit of fun I think) and the cows chase the calves and we all end up getting a bit bad-tempered. There's a lot of footpaths over my land and you get people walking through the fields of cows and calves with their dogs running loose. I suppose they know they're risking their lives?' he said, leaning back and yawning.

'Well, maybe not their lives, but they're certainly risking their limbs, Mmmm.'

Pigs are not dirty animals at all, in Eddie's opinion. 'If they have a chance to keep themselves clean, they will. They always use a certain part of the pen to make their mess in . . . as long as they're happy that is. If, for some reason, they are disturbed or get in a draught, which they hate, they will mess all over the pen then. I don't know why. You'd think that that would just make them even more uncomfortable, wouldn't you?'

Eddie Ireton brings his pigs in at ten or twelve weeks old, and keeps them for about twenty weeks before they go for meat. They might arrive two hundred at a time, all mixed up together, and then they would be divided into different pens, where, according to Eddie 'they may fratch a bit' because it is all new to them, but it's not serious. However, having been together in the same pen for a while, if you tried to put two pens of pigs together, they would keep to their separate groups and fight one another in earnest.

'They will defend their own pen,' Eddie said, 'and so if you found one pig running about loose and put it back in the wrong pen by mistake, the other pigs there would kill it. Now, I don't think they recognise a pig that doesn't belong by sight. I think it must be their highly developed sense of smell that tells them it came from a different pen. Pigs have very good hearing, too. If you were to go into the building and they were all grunting about and you just tapped a tin with a stick, they would be dead quiet: for just about a minute it would be so quiet in there that you wouldn't know there was an animal in the place.'

After their evening feed, the pigs drink a lot of water and then they settle down for the night.

'By that time the floor will be completely clean. They leave it absolutely spotless,' Eddie said. 'Then they all go to sleep in a heap, all snuggled up. It must be quite fun, really,' he said, with a hint of a smile.

Eddie does not recall any particular pig that has passed through his hands during his years of farming any more than he remembers any particular cow or sheep. But he does feel that a good farmer should *get among* his animals, because cattle 'and that' are like plants who have to be looked after to get the harvest.

'If a farmer were to keep only pigs,' said Eddie, 'he would have to be turning four thousand or so through a year to make a living out of them. You might make a profit of £4 or £5 a pig, but you would be very lucky if you made that much every time. Once they are ready to go, you have to sell them regardless because if you keep them on they'll get fat, and then they will drop down a grade which means you get less money for them.'

Pigs are graded for fatness after they have been killed.

'They are graded on a backfat probe,' Eddie said. 'They use an instrument like the thing you use to measure the tread on your car tyres, and that tells them how much fat is on there. For Top Grade you are looking for 17mm of fat – that's not much fat, is it? We are trying to produce long, lean pigs, but they don't all finish out that way.'

In Eddie's opinion the presence of the pigs on his farm benefits the other animals because the slurry they produce is used to fertilise the grass for the cattle and sheep.

'It's another by-product, if you like,' Eddie said. 'It helps to keep the grass growing. It's a big help, because it's very high in nitrogen content. You have to look after your land before it will look after you, Mmmm.'

And why do the pigs not have curly tails any more? Eddie explained that they are cut when the pigs are small to prevent 'tail-biting'. What's that?

'Those pigs out there,' Eddie said patiently. 'I don't think they're unhappy, but it must get a bit boring for them, mustn't it? There they are in the pen, hour after hour, watching these tails go by in front of their faces.' He waved his forefinger backwards and forwards in front of his nose to show what it must be like. 'So, one day, they decide to have a nip. And once they've tried it and tasted blood, there's no stopping them: they'll keep on biting. So the tails are cut short to stop all that.'

Later that evening Eddie walked into the local pub. In a crowded bar, Eddie Ireton is the sort of man who gets served almost before he is through the door. Another local farmer greeted him as he stood at the bar:

'Edward. How's it going?'

Eddie acknowledged him with a nod.

25

'Pretty fair,' he said, amiably. Farmers keep their troubles to themselves.

'We try to keep up with the times,' he told me. 'Financially we have to. I paid 2,500 guineas for a Limousin bull because they produce leaner meat than the Hereford bulls we've always had in the past. That is what people want these days. It's the same with pigs. Nobody wants fat pigs any more, Mmmm.' He took a swig of his beer. 'I rent a bit of land. When you feel you're doing a bit of something for yourself, it seems to help the job along. So you buy sheep and you buy cattle; but to do that, you have to have something to sell, haven't you? Farmers these days have all got overdrafts. In the past if you owed the bank £400 you would have thought you were in a bad way, but I know farmers today who are in debt for more like half a million. It's a millstone round their necks. Some farmers spend their lives just working off the interest on the money they've borrowed to buy a place, so that some day, eventually, that land will belong to some member of their family. It's what you might call a long-term investment,' Eddie said with a rueful smile.

The pheasant shooting season ends on 31st January, and the last event of the season is usually a shoot for the beaters who have been 'putting up' the birds for the guns all winter. The Beaters' Day is very often a 'cocks only' shoot because the keeper wants to limit their numbers. He explained, sounding exasperated by their stupidity, that if there are too many male birds among those left to breed in the wild, 'they spend all their time fighting one another, and not enough time breeding.' As soon as the last shot has been fired, the keeper begins to catch up his surviving pheasants to put them in the laying pens where they will mate in March, and the female birds will then lay their eggs in April.

Catching up pheasants is a job Bob Carter, the keeper, prefers to do alone. Only he knows where the birds will be feeding and that is not the sort of information he wants to broadcast. All winter long Bob has been walking the woods, whistling up his birds for food and scattering grain for them in quiet corners. The wild birds too, benefit from his efforts.

'It's the little birds that come off worst in bad weather,' he said. 'It's the wrens, the tits and the chaffinches. A hard winter leaves hundreds dead. There's nothing for them to eat and, when they're weakened by hunger, the hawks get them.'

The keeper catches his birds in wooden or wire cages which he leaves in the pheasants' regular feeding places. The way in is a wire funnel, the bait is the food and, once they are in, the pheasants cannot find the way out. Every few days the 'catchers' are moved to a different site.

'I usually do that job at night,' Bob said. 'I don't want everyone to know what I'm up to.'

Once the catchers are set the keeper goes round each one every few hours to pick up the birds caught inside. He arrives with a sack, opens the catcher, and moving slowly so as not to alarm the birds any more than is necessary, reaches inside, talking all the time: 'Come here, come along, you little pillock.' The birds are picked up by their wings but close to the body so that there is no risk of injury. As Bob straightens up with a pheasant in his hand, he gives it a quick, critical look-over before it goes into the sack. The colours of the cock birds are even more striking seen close to: gleaming russet or kingfisher-blue feathers on the heads and breasts giving way to downy brown and speckled colouring over the legs. The keeper turns the birds upside-down for a look at the legs: the spurs just above the feet are a good indication of the age of the birds, and age is one of the considerations to be taken into account when the keeper makes his final selection of birds for the laying pens. Once all the birds are in the sack, the keeper takes them back to his van. It is an odd experience to walk behind a man with a sackful of heaving pheasants over his shoulder. Lumps appear and disappear and small, protesting noises can be heard. From a small hole in the sack the sleek head of a cock pheasant emerges – dark, round, unblinking eyes ringed with dazzling white, staring imperiously at the world from his swaying porthole three feet from the ground.

27

The keeper will begin with one cock bird to every six hens in the laying pens and the cock birds are carefully selected.

'You don't want anything too old,' Bob said. 'By the time they're three years old their spurs will have grown to about half or three-quarters of an inch long, so they can injure the hens when they jump on them: they slash them down the sides. They're more like fighting cocks at that age.'

The ratio of male birds to females will eventually drop to one male to eight females by natural selection . . . well, not entirely natural.

'Some of the male birds seem shy or frightened or something,' said Bob. 'They hide themselves away in the corners all the time. They're no good.' The shy ones do not last long; they get weeded out by the keeper and knocked sharply on the head.

February can be a difficult month for moving tractors into the fields because of the damage they do to the wet land, but farmers with large areas to cover can call in an 'ag flyer' to fertilise their crops for them, weather permitting.

An 'agricultural pilot' flies low over the fields and then, at the last minute, climbs steeply away in order to clear the neighbouring houses or trees. An aircraft with a 36-foot wingspan looks very large when it appears directly over your chimney-pot. Bob Sharp is an 'ag pilot' and his aeroplane is a Piper Pawnee 235 horsepower single-seater, which is the smallest aircraft used for agricultural flying, but, according to Bob Sharp, the best for conditions where the fields are small and there are houses, trees, high-tension cables and telephone wires close by.

For spreading fertiliser the plane has to be reloaded every ten minutes. The load carried depends on how good a site the farmer has been able to provide for landing and taking off.

'You always load a little bit less than you think you are going to get off with,' Bob Sharp said laconically.

He is a very cool customer indeed, slightly mocking, dismissive of danger. While he was taking off for the first run of the day over a bumpy, grass-covered field, the conversation between the farmer who had hired him and a passer-by cut out in mid-sentence as the plane remained earthbound for what seemed a long, long time.

'He always does get off in the end,' the farmer said with a nervous laugh. He did.

With large areas to fertilise the aircraft is left overnight on its makeshift landing-strip and that apparently can have its hazards. Before taking off Bob had been having a particularly good look at the cowlings on the engine: Why?

'When we're not about, people come to have a look,' he said, 'and they just can't resist taking a peep at the engine. But they never know how to do the cowlings up again, so if they're not fixed properly, you know somebody's been piddling around with your aeroplane.'

The minimum requirementss for a landing site are about 300 yards in which to land and about 500 yards in which to take off.

'As for the surface,' Bob Sharp said, 'we reckon that if you can drive a car or a Land Rover over it at 20 miles per hour, it's good enough.'

For flying the cloud base has to be above 500 feet and the visibility one nautical mile. The fertiliser is then loaded into a hopper in the nose of the plane and then released into a spreader underneath. At the back of the spreader, the granules ping off the reflector plates which spread them out as they shoot away. The fields to be spread with fertiliser will have been staked out by Bob Sharp or his partner with red, orange and yellow markers which act as guides, so that the pilot can fly between them and spread the fertiliser in strips.

Before he flies, Bob Sharp is given a map of the area and a worksheet, prepared by his partner, with a note of any special hazards. After that, it is up to him, with the map on his knee, to do the job in a way that causes minimum nuisance to the population.

'The way to make people grumble about you is to make it look hairy,' he said. 'We are up against people who think we are cowboys, and environmentalists who run about after us trying to get sprayed, so that they can complain. It is always better to come in over a property and fly away from it, than to fly towards a house,

29

cut off the spray just short of the garden and pull up over the house. People don't like you zapping across their chimney pots at low-level.'

It is a mistake to compare agricultural flying with stunt flying when talking to an ag pilot. They do not like it.

'Stunt flying is done much higher up with more space to play with,' Bob Sharp explained tersely, 'It is done for effect and probably puts more stress on the pilot and on his aircraft than agricultural flying, which is precision flying. Ag pilots have to be able to place their planes to the nearest foot – up, down or sideways. The last thing we want to be is spectacular.

Later in the year when the liquid fungicides and insecticides are sprayed onto the crops and the pilots have to fly at two or three feet over the ground because liquid sprays are more likely to drift in the wind, such precision is no easy task.

If people on the ground do get upset and shout and swear, it does not bother Bob Sharp because he cannot hear them . . . he cannot hear anything at all because the noise of the engine is so loud. He tried wearing a walkman once, turned up to full volume, but he could not even hear that. Does this constant noise not bother him at all?

'It would bother me if it stopped,' he said.

Within range of an airport, he is required by law to stay tuned in to Aircraft Control.

'When I'm in the middle of a spray run, travelling at one hundred miles per hour and just about to fly under some telephone wires, it doesn't help when they call me up to tell me to keep a look out for a helicopter two miles away at 500 feet flying from east to west,' he said. 'I could do without that.'

But the main problem for the agricultural pilot is people. 'We've all been shot at,' Bob said casually. 'You're not aware of it when it happens, but many a time you find shot-gun pellets in the aircraft when you land. Some people are dedicated to getting spraying abolished and unfortunately aerial work like this has a high profile.'

There is one lady in the south of England who will not allow any aerial spraying within a mile of her property. She is so well-known that she is marked on the maps of all the ag pilots. 'We do our best not to add insult to injury,' Bob Sharp said, 'but you have to bear in mind that the farmer is paying to have his fields sprayed. One pilot saw this woman pointing a gun at him and he rather took it to heart. He landed the 'plane and rang the police to report her. They went round and discovered her in the garden pointing a broomstick at the sky. It wasn't a gun at all. The police asked us if we'd like to prosecute her for causing a distraction which could have been dangerous, but we declined,' he said, smiling gently.

There is a widely-held belief that ag pilots can only work for two years before they crack up under the strain, but Bob Sharp said that he had never known of anyone who cracked up, unless they were unsuited to the job in the first place. He explained that you do have to be a steady sort of person: it is forward planning that makes an agricultural pilot successful rather than quick reactions. Bob himself has been ag flying for seventeen years. He liked the look of the job when he first saw it because it seemed to be something exciting and special, but he did his first spray jobs in Africa because to work in England you have to have a minimum of 500 ag flying hours under your belt.

Standing in the village street later in the day, an old man leaning on his walking stick watched Bob Sharp zooming overhead on a turn between runs.

'He'll be top-dressing the corn, I expect,' the man said. 'I used to do that by hand forty years ago. We used to spread one hundred-weight per acre for a shilling. Those were good days,' he mused. 'We thought so, anyway.'

MARCH

Here comes March in full sail. Huge clouds move across the sky, deceptively serene, as a gale is battering and booming at everything in its path at ground level. Small birds try to keep to cover, but occasionally a small shape zig-zags its way through the air, making for shelter as quickly as possible. Only the seagulls sweep unconcernedly across the fields where the winter corn is growing thick and green, only distinguishable from grass to the casual eye by the narrow, straight lines of earth between the new growth. An empty, blue fertiliser bag cartwheels across the middle of a field. Like an ever-enthusiastic new broom March sends rubbish flying and bangs with frantic energy on anything not firmly nailed down.

In a temporary lull we emerge, shriven, in a newly laundered world. At first glance there is not much to see, but the catkins are wriggling with delight on the hazel trees: maybe there is more going on than we know. Richard Jefferies thought so:

> Let the cold be never so great or the sky so clouded . . . that
> the mysterious influence of the light, as the sun slowly rises
> higher in the meridian, sinks into the earth like a magic rain.
> It enters the hardest bark and the rolled-up bud, so firm that
> its points will prick the finger like a thorn; it stirs beneath
> the surface of the ground. A magnetism that is not heat, and
> for which there is no exact name, works out of sight in
> answer to the sun.

A more careful look at the earth under the clanking, creaking branches of a coppice reveals fragile green shoots that can be seen forcing their way through last year's débris. The influence of the light has called them, and they are coming; pushing aside stones and soil and dead leaves with infinite insistence. Fixed of purpose, an invincible green army will soon take possession of the woodland floor.

> . . . *And one green spear*
> *Stabbing a dead leaf from below*
> *Kills winter at a blow.*

(Andrew Young, *Last Snow*)

The busiest times of the year in the cattle markets are in spring and autumn when, apart from the regular sales of fat stock and barren cows, more young animals are coming onto the market. Gloucester Cattle Market attracts stock from all over the Midlands and Wales, and buyers from even further afield.

The market begins at nine-thirty in the morning. Trucks full of animals follow one another into the market area and lower their ramps, spilling out cows, sheep and pigs into the concrete alleyways between the pens where the animals wait for their turn to be sold. There are drovers helping to guide the animals into separate pens. I watched as a sudden flurry of sheep came along an alleyway, followed by a drover in a green overall and a bad temper.

'Come back!' he shouted. 'Stay there!'

It seemed a lot to ask of a flock of strange sheep in a state of panic. As the sheep rushed past me I realised, too late, that he had been shouting at me.

'I thought you was stood there, stopping them,' he puffed resentfully as he ran past.

The first event of the day is the calf sale. Round a small ring the buyers stand shoulder to shoulder while one calf at a time comes in through a door at the side of the auctioneer's rostrum and, once sold, goes out through a door at the other side. The calves were between one and two weeks old. The man standing next to me bought a heifer calf for £50.

'I'm an opportunist,' he said. 'I usually find they go that little bit cheaper in the first half hour, so I take my chance.'

He told me that he owned a farm near Ledbury; 60 acres of land on which he kept 150 ewes and grew about 25 acres of corn, but he liked to have a few cattle to graze through the summer.

'If you need a quid or two in a hurry, you can always sell one of them,' he said. 'It's an insurance policy.'

He was buying heifer calves because they were going for half the price of bull calves.

'They're not cheap, but they are less money,' he said. 'You have to take into account that at twelve weeks old a heifer is going to be worth something like £130 while a bull calf, which puts on more weight, might be worth £230.'

The auctioneer announced that the calf being sold belonged to a farmer who was at the ringside. He was obviously well known and well respected because the calf reached a good price. I watched his face as it was finally knocked down to a buyer. Was he pleased?

'We've got to be pleased, haven't we?' he said, moving away to collect his cheque from the office, and not looking pleased at all.

The auctioneer was hammering on at a tremendous speed: he needed to, not only to get through all the calves that were due to be sold, but to keep his buyers' attention. Calf dealers are a disorderly lot, especially when they get together.

'Here we have one heifer,' the auctioneer said, as another calf came into the ring.

'It's a bull,' shouted the buyers in unison.

'Oh yes,' said the auctioneer. He picked up a piece of paper and read out what it said: 'Please note that the discoloured eye has been treated and should not give any trouble.'

'Oh, that's nice!' shouted the buyers. The bidding started again:

'Fifty, on two, on four, on six, on eight, to my left . . . Now's your chance, on eight . . . What's the matter with you? . . .'

The buyers made their bids by raising their hands or nodding at the auctioneer: bidding requires concentration but the calf dealers still found time to talk.

'Good calves, these, aren't they?' one of them called to another across the ring.

'Good 'uns? Look at the feet on that one, Bernard.'

Another calf came into the ring and one of the dealers leaned over to explain to me that this one was no good.

'No shoulders,' he explained. 'Hips sticking up. He's got no shape: what you want is a square sort of a calf. That one's got nothing behind – from the hocks to the top of the tail, there's nothing there. There's never going to be no meat on him.' The calf was a Holstein. 'They brought them in because they produce a lot of milk,' the dealer continued, 'but they never thought about the calves, did they? And it's quality we want now in milk, not quantity, so it's rebounded on them. We want British calves, not this foreign rubbish.'

Several calves had come and gone during this explanation and the man who was talking shouted out a bid just a second after the auctioneer had knocked down the last one. The auctioneer hesitated for a second and then decided to ignore him.

'Bloody hell, look up will you, Charlie?' the dealer shouted at him in frustration.

One of his friends, standing next to him, laughed.

'You nearly upset the applecart there, Jack, didn't you?' he said. Jack turned to me and said, 'We're spending a King's Ransom in here. We need a bit of light relief.'

Behind the auctioneer's rostrum the calves still to be sold were waiting in their pens. A young woman with long hair was leaning over one pen looking closely at a small, pathetic looking calf.

'I could do something with him,' she said. 'They are called Bobby calves, the weedy-looking ones. I like to keep a few and watch them grow. If you feed them by hand they get very affectionate and I hate having to sell them. It hurts, but it hurts my purse even more to try and keep them when they get too big. If you can buy a calf at the right price and then calculate the cost of the feed on top of that, it is the only thing I know of that will grow into money . . . but not much money.'

A bell sounded in the distance and she sprang to her feet like Cinderella on the stroke of midnight.

'I've got to go,' she said. 'They're selling my goat.'

Further over in the market the sheep sale had started: a much more sedate affair, there was no heckling from the sheep men. Next

36

in line were the pigs, waiting, squealing in their pens, and right at the end of the market was the 'Deadstock Sale'. In spite of its ominous name this is where the farmers bring any spare produce they have to sell. In season there are flowers and plants, fruit trees and fencing, potatoes by the sackful, cabbages, and enormous quantities of eggs, including boxes of pale-blue, green and pink duck eggs and goose eggs marked 'Picked up fresh this morning. Should be fertile.' The Deadstock Market is where an auctioneer will begin his career. The people bidding for flowers, fruit and eggs are not so unruly, or so tense.

'The secret of being a good auctioneer,' said John Lawrence, a partner in Gloucester Market Auctioneers, 'is to be a good valuer. If you start the bidding at the wrong price, you're going to waste time.'

There is no time to waste with so many animals moving through the market. In the fatstock ring Mike Credland gets through about two hundred and fifty beasts in two hours, with each animal spending only about twelve seconds actually in the ring before being sold. The fatstock sale was the last to start and the last to finish. One difficulty about this side of the business, John Lawrence explained, is that 'fat' is now a dirty word. The general public does not like it. So the stock are now described as being 'well-furnished lean steers' and these will get a better price than the 'thick steer which is over-finished' or, in other words, fat.

By two o'clock in the afternoon, Mike Credland's 'flu was getting him down, but his buyers were in high spirits. The animals came into the ring over a weighbridge and their weight was shown up in lights on a digital display over the auctioneer's rostrum. The buyers bid in pence per kilo, which is difficult to follow, even if you can see who was bidding. By the time the sale was nearing its end, the buyers were standing in clusters round the ring, talking to one another and bidding at the same time.

'Who's winning?' a buyer shouted at Mike Credland.

'You want to wake up,' Mike Credland told him.

Each bid is repeated in a long, unbroken chant until the hammer bangs down and a steel gate crashes shut behind the animal as it leaves the ring.

Over a glass of squash after the auction was over, Mike Credland explained, between bouts of blowing his nose, that only the auctioneer can really see where the bids are coming from.

'Some people move their hands, some wink and some nod. Everyone has their own way of making a bid and it's all very discreet. I had a father and son at the ringside once, but there was a man standing between them. They were both bidding for the same beast, but they didn't know it.' He snorted with laughter and blew his nose again.

By three o'clock in the afternoon the market is emptying with almost miraculous speed. The drovers are busy pushing and heaving the cattle, sheep and pigs up the ramps of the transporters which will take them to their new homes.

'Come along little ones,' a forceful-looking woman said in a voice ringing with authority as she opened a pen where six calves were waiting.

The calves skittered around her, good as gold, like puppies, as she walked down the alleyway. A drover who had just had the devil's own job with a calf which did not want to go where he was taking it, looked on dourly.

'Good with calves, women are,' he said. 'I suppose it's the old maternal instinct coming out, isn't it?' He made it sound like an insult.

There is nothing quite so bleak and empty as a cattle market when everyone has gone. The clashing of the last metal gate behind the last cow, the muffled bang of the last door thumping shut on the cattle trucks echo dismally in the silence. As I walked away I caught up with an old farmer who was making his way slowly towards the road. He had been after a couple of young beasts to fatten up on the grazing, but he had not found anything at the market that day to suit his pocket. He told me that everyone was telling him he should retire. His wife was all for moving into a bungalow, but farming was all he knew and he did not want to give up, not yet.

'I hope the people who do the planning in this country know what they are doing,' he said, as he pointed to the dual carriageway where traffic was moving in both directions in an endless stream. 'They're forever making these new roads and car parks and hypermarkets. I hope they realise that people will still be living here a thousand years from now and it's land they will need. If they keep on concreting over the countryside at the rate they're going now, there'll be nothing left for the farmers and without farmers there'd be no food for folks, would there?'

In March there is a tremendous hullaballoo going on at the top of the trees where the rooks are renovating their nests. Rooks appear to build by committee and the finished results look like a case of too many rooks spoiling the broth! But in spite of appearances the nests are well-enough constructed to last from one year to the next, and to withstand the dizzying swaying of the branches in the wind, although from the ground a rookery looks just like a collection of witches' handbags dumped between the long black fingers of the tree-tops. In March it is the big, messy nests that catch the eye, but they are all too far off the ground to run the risk of being plundered. The smaller birds weave their snug nests in secret, far from prying eyes in evergreen bushes, ivy-covered trees and hidden crevices. The tree-top builders can afford to be more casual, but it is a mystery how the pigeon population ever survives the off-hand efforts of the parent birds who build flimsy little platforms of sticks across a couple of slender branches – so insubstantial that, from below, you can see right through them.

The untidy heaps of broken twigs wedged in the forks of trees are not fallen birds' nests, but squirrels' dreys, and the sight of them, bulging against the bark, brings a gleam to the eyes of John Hammond. His war against the grey squirrel – 'those vermin' as he calls them – hots up at this time of year, when the young are in the nests. Although the dreys serve as shelters for the squirrels during the winter (grey squirrels do not hibernate in the true sense of the word), not all the dreys will be in use in March. Walking through the woods with John Hammond I asked him how he could tell which dreys were inhabited.

'Watch this,' he said.

He went up to a tall, slim tree, put his arms round the trunk and shook it. It is surprising how much movement can be produced by shaking a tree – enough to startle a squirrel anyway. A grey shape shot out of the drey above our heads, leapt into an adjoining tree and disappeared behind the trunk. Jackpot! John Hammond bent down to pick up his hat which had fallen off in all the excitement.

'See that mole run there?' he said. 'Did you know that every mole has its own territory and at mating time the male mole has to make his way to the female mole who is only on heat for about forty-eight hours? So if you see a mole run going in a straight line, you can be sure that that was a male mole in a hurry. Unfortunately for the mole, if he arrives too early or too late, the female bites him on the nose and that kills him.'

The salmon fishing season on the Tyne river in Northumbria lasts from the beginning of February to the end of October for rods, but on 26th March the season opens for netting salmon from licensed fishing boats. The river Tyne is associated in the minds of most people with the stretch from Newcastle to the sea, where shipbuilders and a variety of industries line its banks, but strenuous efforts in pollution control by the local Water Authority have succeeded in making the Tyne one of the finest rivers for salmon and trout in the country. I talked to a spokesman for the British Field Sports Society and he told me.

'Salmon are one of the most sensitive fish to pollution. If you get salmon coming up through the industrialised part of the river to the headwater, you know you're making progress.'

But where there are salmon to be caught, there will be poachers trying to catch them, so to protect the salmon, bailiffs are appointed by the Water Authority.

The head water-bailiff for the Tyne is a man called Ivan Swaile; a quiet, softly-spoken man who looks – in his green jacket and cords, with neat fair hair and very clean fingernails – like a successful businessman on a day out in the country. We met in Hexham to drive to Howden where the Fisheries Protection launch is moored, and on the way he explained that apart from these routine patrols he was also responsible for the whole of the Tyne, which including all its tributaries amounts to well over three hundred miles of water, most of it in wild, remote country as the North Tyne rises in the Cheviot Hills and the South Tyne in the Pennines. Since becoming head water-bailiff Ivan Swaile has walked every inch of that river and its tributaries.

'They all end up in my river,' he said, 'every one of them. I don't think you would find a river with so many tributaries anywhere in the country.'

Every day he walks and drives around some part of his beat in order to make 'a presence felt'. But what is this gentle man doing tackling gangs of unscrupulous poachers, sometimes single-handed, and getting his nose broken?

'We all have that bit fear,' he said; but the answer is that he loves his river. Water-bailiffs have the power to arrest anybody taking or attempting to take fish from a river 'in contravention of the Salmon and Freshwater Fisheries Act, 1957'. In fact a water-bailiff has all the powers and privileges of a police constable, as long as it is dark. The law states that they can arrest any poacher 'during the period commencing one hour after sunset and ending one hour before sunrise'. Why is that?

'I'd very much like to know myself,' Ivan said mildly.

The only slight improvement as far as the bailiffs are concerned has been the passing of the Police and Criminal Evidence Act, which came into force in January 1986, whereby a water-bailiff can arrest anyone who is thought to have given a false name and address, even in the hours of daylight.

'They come in groups, you see,' Ivan said, 'so we have to try to separate them and then, when they've given us their names and addresses, we ask one of them what he calls the others and see if he slips up.'

From January, when the salmon start coming in from the sea, to the end of the year, when they reach the headwaters where they will spawn, Ivan Swaile knows that there will be people trying to catch them 'by fair means or foul'. The water-bailiffs get to know every man licensed to fish on the river – several thousand of them every year.

'Of course there are always those who think that they can get away with a bit of fishing in a quiet spot without going through the bother and expense of getting themselves a licence: but they can't,' said Ivan. 'Not on my river.'

In the last ten years Ivan has seen the numbers of fish increase.

'Even the otters are making a small comeback,' he added, 'although there are still only a couple of pair on the whole Tyne system as far as I could tell from the footprints I found last winter. And the seals are now coming up as far as the tidal water runs, fifteen miles up river from the sea.'

But there have been losses too. Mink are widespread in Northumberland, either having escaped from captivity or having been released by misguided do-gooders.

'The mink have devastated the water voles, those harmless vegetarians,' Ivan said, 'and they've destroyed the water hens too. We have to try to keep a balance on the river. We try to trap a few mink when we've time, but the problem is too widespread for us to make any real impact on it.'

Ivan Swaile's hobby is birdwatching, although he regards this as almost part of the job.

'You can only judge your river by how the wildlife is being affected,' he said. 'If the goosanders, herons and cormorants are on the increase there must be fish for them to eat. When the wildlife starts to decline, then you know you're in trouble.'

In September and October there is a law against fishing for salmon 100 metres below an artificial or a natural obstruction, to give the fish a chance to reach the head of the rivers to spawn.

'But wherever the fish go, the poachers will be there,' Ivan said, 'with their nets or their rods, or in the spawning grounds with their gaffs (barbed hooks) and lamps. The poachers are like predators. They will take the risks when they are going to make most money. Poaching gangs have been caught with 73 fish of around 25 pounds each in weight, and if you know how much a pound of fresh salmon would cost you, you can work out how much they stand to gain if they can get away with it. These people are not out for one for the pot.'

As far as the poachers tackled by the Fisheries Protection launch, *The Three Rivers*, were concerned, there was a great deal of money involved.

'One gang that was taken recently had two boats confiscated and one of those was a trawler valued at twenty thousand pounds,' Ivan said. 'And apart from the boats they had two cars with them, both Volvos.'

We arrived at Howden and drew up on the quayside. There was nothing in sight.

'The boat's down there,' Ivan said.

I looked over the side and a long way down there was *The Three Rivers*, tied up and heaving at the quayside. The only way down was an iron ladder attached to the wall. Had I told Ivan about my morbid fear of deep water? I glanced at him and saw that he was waiting politely for me to swing myself out into space and precede him down the ladder. This was obviously not the moment to mention it.

On the deck of the 'Boowat' as Ivan called it, there was the skipper of *The Three Rivers*, Jimmy Flett, waiting to welcome us. Jimmy Flett was a cheerful young man wearing bright-blue overalls and bright-yellow rubber gloves which he took off to shake hands and put on again to go down and start the engine.

The Three Rivers is 48 feet long and has a 300-horsepower engine. It can go anywhere from six feet of water to deep sea, and, apart from the river, has a stretch of coastline twelve miles long and stretching six miles out to sea to patrol.

'We're a deterrent, aren't we, Ivan?' Jimmy said when he had returned to the wheelhouse and pulled off his rubber gloves which were embarrassing him by their brightness.

Jimmy admits that he prefers the patrolling to the 'aggro'. At sea, when there might be a boat poaching salmon Jimmy Flett can pin-point its position by a combination of navigational aids, making a top hat effect on his chart by collating information from his Decca Navigator, his radar, and his depth indicator, and by taking bearings from landmarks on the coast. He also has a digi-scanner in the wheelhouse which whips through all the radio channels in the area and automatically picks up anything on the local airwaves.

'We can hear the gangs talking to one another,' he said. 'The first thing we hear them say is that they've seen us coming and after that I can't tell you what they say because it's unprintable.'

Jimmy Flett explained that the best weather for catching poachers is either thick fog or a very dark night, when the lights on *The Three Rivers* sometimes 'accidentally failed' as they moved in on a suspected poacher. Jimmy Flett has a list of all the licensed salmon fishermen in his area – all 121 of them – and part of his job is to make sure that they are not using nets longer than the legal 600 yards. If there is any doubt he has to tie up alongside, get the nets hauled in and measure them by hand with a six foot pole . . . 'which is a very tedious job'.

According to Jimmy Flett, this trip was to be a routine patrol of the river. The sort of poacher they were looking for was the industrial worker who drops a net into the river and leaves it there while he gets on with his shift in the factory.

'Ivan's your man for that; he's practically put a stop to that by now,' Jimmy said, explaining that it takes very good eyesight to spot a net floating at the side of a busy river.

'But if you know what you're looking for, you can spot the floats,' he went on.

'Or a rope attached to the side and dangling into the water,' said Ivan.

'But with binoculars I can guarantee to tell you exactly what they've caught,' Jimmy said, 'just by watching the way they haul in the net.'

In a place called 'the Gut', where a lot of small boats tie up, Ivan and Jimmy had recently arrested a gang who had just come back with a big haul of fish, and one of the poachers had taken a knife to them.

'I would say you always have to be wary,' Jimmy said. 'It's no good being frightened because if you're frightened you might let one of your mates down. We all have our own jobs to do: Ivan organises that. He's your man for organising. We all know exactly what we've to do. It's a case of split-second timing, you see, because if you hash it up the gang will ditch the fish. They just throw them away and dead salmon sink and that's your evidence gone.'

When the water-bailiffs take poachers to court they only have their own account of what happened and any fish or nets they have confiscated to produce as evidence.

'But if the men have a history of poaching, their past convictions are read out in court and then they get clatter,' Ivan said.

The big-time poachers Ivan and Jimmy have caught in the past do not forget and they certainly do not forgive.

'I had a group of VIP's on the boat recently,' Jimmy Flett said, 'and when I had seen them safely back on shore, a man who we'd taken to court happened to come along, and just as I was climbing down the ladder from the quayside, he tried to kick me in the face, and me all in my bonny gear too.'

About half the sugar consumed in Britain is produced from homegrown sugar-beet, mostly grown in the Midlands and Eastern counties where the soil suits this particular crop. Sugar-beet can only be grown on contract. The local processors who have set up their factories in the Eastern counties sign up the farmers to produce a certain tonnage the following season at an agreed price, providing that the crop has the required percentage of sugar content. Alan Riddlestone farms 70 acres of land near Colchester, Essex, and grows sugar-beet in rotation with wheat and barley. The farm was bought by his grandfather a hundred years ago and paid for, according to family legend, with gold sovereigns.

'My grandfather, Old Fred, couldn't read or write and he signed his name with a cross, but you couldn't fiddle him out of a farthing,' Alan Riddlestone told me.

Alan is a big, active man with a weather-beaten face, huge hands and an air of quiet authority. He typifies the changes that have taken place in the countryside over the past generation: whereas when his grandfather was in charge, the farm was almost self-sufficient with a couple of house cows kept for milk, three or four sows for breeding, half a dozen bullocks grazing the rough ground and chickens running about everywhere, there is no livestock there today. In the past there were plenty of people to help with the work, but today Alan Riddlestone works the farm single-handed.

'It's a lonely life,' he said, 'although it's child's play with a combine.'

Keeping livestock doesn't make sense for a man with 70 acres of good arable land and no help, but he was sorry to see the stock go. To him, and hundreds of farmers like him: 'a farm is not a farm without animals. It's just a prairie.' Alan would have liked to have kept calves. 'But when calves need an injection, they need it yesterday; tomorrow is too late.'

So, like the shrewd man he is, and all farmers like to think they are shrewd, he stuck to his crops. But he looks back to the old days with affection.

'There was time to take a pride in your work then,' he said. 'Today it's all rush.'

A good crop of sugar-beet can be rewarding, but a lot depends on the weather.

'You can do everything right, exactly by the book,' Alan said, 'but in the end, if the rain and the sun don't come at the right time, you won't get your results. The Master is up there all the time,' he said, glancing at the sky.

Weather permitting, Alan Riddlestone likes to get his sugar-beet sown between 24th March and 10th April. He likes to plant early to give the seeds a better root hold in the light soil.

'You need a fine seedbed for sowing sugar-beet,' he said, 'a nice, even, smooth bed like a flower-bed. A "filth of tilth" as we call it,' he said, with a deep, rich chuckle.

He sows his seed with a precision drill pulled behind his tractor. The drill has a conveyor belt with seed-pellet-sized holes in it so that a seed drops through every seven inches. He 'drills to stand', which means that he doesn't have to go back and thin them out later on.

'Farming is all about timing,' he explained. 'You have to pick the right day for drilling (planting), otherwise you're in trouble. If it rains heavily just after you've planted your seeds, the soil can become "capped" so the seedlings can't get through. The only solution if that happens is to plough them all up and start again with a new batch of seed.'

Alan Riddlestone can remember his father and grandfather talking about the different sounds the birds made when it was going to rain.

' "Don't like the sound of that," they would say, "damned old thing",' he told me. 'I can't tell the difference myself, so I have to rely on the radio forecasts. But I do know that when it's going to rain the Church bell has a dull note to it. That's a wet old bell,' he said.

Once the seeds start to germinate they need rain.

'There's an old saying that "A dripping June puts things in tune",' said Alan, 'but June's too late. We must have rain in May, followed by showers in June.'

A drought at that time of year could mean a drop in yield from 15 to 8 tons per acre at harvest time.

Another decision to be made is what sprays to use on the crop.

'I know some farmers do what the computer tells them and spray for everything just in case,' Alan said, 'but I spray for what's there. I wait to see what comes up.'

There are a bewildering number of sprays on the market both pre-emergent and post-emergent. Alan Riddlestone will never forget one he tried in the past which had to be applied and then harrowed in within fifteen minutes. It meant driving down the field on one tractor with the spray, then jumping onto another tractor and driving back to harrow it in.

'I thought I was going mad,' he said.

He decided that if that was the last word in modern technology, he could do without it.

Alan Riddlestone gets his advice about what to spray and when from a representative of an agricultural spraying company.

'And at the end of the day,' he said, 'what I want to know is how many pints per acre I should use, and the man gets out his calculator and tells me.'

As chemicals come in five-litre containers with instructions for applying them worked out in hectares, farm-workers these days are far more likely to be carrying a metric conversion table than a pitchfork.

APRIL

The country habit has me by the heart
For he's bewitched forever who has seen
Not with his eyes, but with his vision, Spring
Flow down the woods and stipple leaves with sun.
(V. Sackville-West, *The Land*)

The signs of spring can arrive under cover of a grey sheet of rain, like ghostly actors taking their places on stage before the lights go up. But whether the sun shines or not, the performance is beginning. It is the lengthening of the days that initiates growth, while the weather controls the amount of growth. In April the spring grass is growing, and with the spring grass come the lambs. A ewe's gestation period is five months and in the dark days of November they are at their most fertile so that the lambs will be born in time for the grass which produces the best and richest milk in the ewes. The actual time when the grass and the lambs are due varies by a few weeks through the country – earlier in the south, later in the north.

New-born lambs have a startled look about them as they scramble after their wool-drenched mothers, wide-eyed and bleating. All winter the sheep, grazing in the pastures, have been quiet, but once the lambs are born, there is a constant anxious bleating from the flock. As James Herriot said, 'The sound of sheep, the sound of spring.'

Sheep farmers, like all farmers, are very competitive people, and they do not like to admit to failure, but the fact is that lambing time is a worrying few weeks for them. Not all the births go smoothly and although every shepherd is glad to see twin lambs, triplets can still be a problem because a ewe has only two teats.

'Lambs are just like children, you know: they like to arrive at

49

night,' an old shepherd said. A man with a small flock can at least keep his eye on them. Stan Hayles keeps fifty ewes and two rams on his fruit farm in Kent.

'I bring the ewes into the field next to the house at lambing time and we even string lights up in the trees,' he said. 'It looks like Christmas. The weather is the problem: you can get a lot of rain in the spring. I try to rig up some sort of shelter for the ewes, but it seems to me that when a ewe is about to lamb she must get very hot, because most ewes make their way to the draughtiest and most exposed place they can find to have their lambs. I've picked up newly born lambs that were lying in puddles and that's no good to them; they're born wet and they need to be dried off as quickly as possible. If all is going well, the birth doesn't take long, but if a ewe is in trouble, I have to do what I can to help. There's no time to send for the vet or anything like that; you have to do it yourself. You've got to be careful – if you see a head showing and a pair of front legs, you have to make sure that it isn't twins, and the head of one and the legs of the other aren't trying to get born at the same time. You're bound to lose some. Every farmer does, but we bury our dead and say nothing.'

Stan keeps his lambs for a year and sells them off the following April.

'At least they see one lot of spring grass, don't they?' he said.

John Burra, who farms 700 acres of upland grazing in Cumbria, has a thousand ewes to lamb, so his system is quite different.

'I like to keep them well spread out when they're lambing, and I like them to stay where they've lambed with as little disturbance as possible,' he said.

In that part of the country each field is surrounded by dry stone walls; there are ten miles of them on John Burra's farm, and they provide some shelter for the sheep. Away from the walls the sheep 'just drift along in front of the wind'. John Burra and his shepherd take it in turns to drive the Land Rover round the flock from dawn to dusk, picking up any casualties as they go. An orphan brought back to the farm is shoved into the skin of a dead lamb (four holes for the legs and a join under the chin tied in a bow with orange baler twine) before being put in a pen with the foster mother in the hope she will accept it. John Burra would prefer to work with the orphans actually *in* the fields if he had time.

'I like to get the ewe into a corner with the lamb and get the dog in close. The ewe will start stamping then because the dog is there. It's the mothering instinct beginning to work, you see: she's wanting to protect that lamb and then you've a chance she'll accept it and let it suckle.'

That is the traditional way of working on the upland farms. High up in the fields there are still the remains of sheep pens where the shepherds stayed with the flock and did their work at lambing time, long before the invention of the tractor or the motor car.

It takes a lot of patience to get a weakly lamb to suckle and some lambs are 'slow to foot' too – slow to get on their feet and get on with it. John Burra and his wife, Diana, have done their share of bottle-rearing. They had sixteen lambs in their kitchen one particular year when there was pneumonia among the flock, but John would rather see a lamb 'mothered on' any time, even if it means spending every available minute of at least one day standing in the sheep pen and pushing the lamb back under the ewe. Every lamb counts. All John Burra's lambs will go to the market in the autumn while the ewes are kept on for lambing next year – 'a flying flock'. Airborne sheep? No, a constant flock of ewes with replacements bought in rather than home bred.

Because a sheep has such a strong maternal instinct towards its own lamb, it makes it difficult to get an orphan accepted, but it does mean that all being well, the sheep will make an excellent mother.

'You might see a lamb on its own if you walk past a field, but usually the sheep will be somewhere nearby, keeping out of sight until you've blown past,' John said. 'Even if the ewe goes away for a while, maybe to get a drink from the beck, it's amazing how she'll always find her way back through the flock to her own lamb.'

If you walk past a field of sheep and lambs you will see clumps of wool lying about on the grass: it has come off the sheep. The sheep are losing condition because they are putting everything into their milk.

'When you see a really bedraggled-looking sheep you can be sure she is making a good job of feeding her lambs,' said John. 'That's what good mothering's all about, isn't it?'

They are certainly doing their duty, these sober matrons, but according to Stan Hayles, who has kept cows and goats and pigs as well as sheep in his time, sheep are the only animals who never play with their young. Healthy young lambs, on the other hand, do not appear to have a care in the world. Tugging at their mothers, racing and jumping and chasing, life is one long game to them. To watch them springing into the air, propelled by sheer exuberance, is worth going a long way to see. They do need a bit of sun, though, to help them sparkle.

A cold, wet spring is hard on the lambs and holds back the growth of new grass, and the higher the farm, the worse the problems. Willie Parker farms 250 acres of grass and 750 acres of heather moorland over 1,000 feet above sea level, near Hexham in Northumbria.

He does not waste his breath complaining about the weather.

'We may swear a bit sometimes,' he said, 'but in the end you just have to get on with it.' But, as he says, he does feel sorry for the lambs. 'Imagine the poor things: they come out of a warm belly straight onto the wet, clarty ground. I've been whispering in the ewes' ears that they should hang on for a bit, but they say they're sick of carrying them.'

Willie is a small, sturdy man with a weatherbeaten face and devilment in his blue eyes; he has the look of a man born to withstand wind and weather.

'Oh aye,' he said. 'We've had a few lambs having to be bottle fed. Not that the ewes died or anything, but sometimes they have something wrong with one of their teats and then, if they've twins, they can't feed the two. They're all titty and no fallah if you know what I mean.'

Willie Parker is not a man to turn his back on any new invention that will help him to keep his flock alive. He does his shepherding now on a three-wheeled motorbike, Japanese made, with low pressure flotation tyres like balloons so that it can travel over the wettest ground without getting stuck.

'We take the food out and ferry the new-born lambs and their mothers back to spend twelve or twenty-four hours getting dried out. Otherwise, in this cold and wet, they'd perish,' Willie said.

He was standing with his back to the fire in his farmhouse kitchen, legs apart, very much the head of the house except he was in his stockinged feet and was wearing one blue sock and one red one. The reason for that was that he'd tipped his bike into a ditch on the moor that morning.

'It sank sideways into four feet of water,' he said, and stopped to consider the incident in retrospect. 'I couldn't help laughing,' he said finally, his face breaking into a slow, broad smile.

'There's nothing to beat shepherding on a horse, though, is there, Willie?' asked a friend of his who had dropped in from Hexham, a great horseman himself.

'I will say,' said Willie, 'that whenever I went out on a horse, we always came back together. On this thing, that is not always the case – not when it runs out of petrol.'

He laughed again. Willie Parker still goes shepherding on a horse when the snow is too deep for the trike: 'It's got longer legs than me.'

For those of us who like to think of shepherding as something picturesque and peaceful, the noisy little red trike does not seem a very attractive innovation. I suggested that it was much more satisfying to see a man shepherding on horseback or walking with his dogs.

'Oh aye?' Willie said, watching his cigarette smoke curl up towards the kitchen ceiling; he did not sound very concerned.

He put on his wellingtons and cap and picked up his stick to go out and see some lambs being loaded up into the trailer to go back on to the moor. Eight lambs and four ewes were loaded up and the bike, driven by one of Willie's sons, roared off with the ewes gazing anxiously over the top of the trailer as they bounced away into the distance. The lambs were all wearing little plastic see-through coats with a hole for the head and four holes for their legs. Another new invention designed to keep the wet off them.

'They're made of very thin plastic,' Willie said. 'As the lambs grow they split off and then you've lots of little bits of plastic drifting about the field to be picked up.'

Immediately surrounding the farm are the pastures where the suckler cows Willie keeps are put out in summer – and the bulls. Willie Parker has two bulls, a Charolais and a Simental.

'My father always used to say "watch the quiet ones, you'll not need telling to watch the other kind",' Willie said.

The grass on the pasture land was showing no sign of growing.

'It's out there somewhere: I know it is,' Willie said. 'But it's still under the bloody ground.'

A late spring means more hard work for Willie and his sons and extra feed for the stock, which all costs money. In summer the cows and bulls go out into the pasture land together or else there would be no calves next year. It is as simple as that. Willie does not favour artificial insemination.

'It seems to me,' he said, 'that with a decent bull on the farm, you get a more uniform product.'

He still has trouble with walkers who leave gates open and get the stock muddled up.

'I think the first one must come along and open the gate and then the next one arrives, sees the gate open and waltzes through without a second thought,' he said.

But what happens if the walkers meet one of his bulls?

'As far as I know the law says that as long as it is not an official footpath, the bull is entitled to the first round,' Willie said. 'Of course there might not be a second,' he added with a grin.

All around the farm the grouse moors stretch away into the distance: 25,000 acres of open land without a single fence. The farms in the area have the right to so many stints of land on the moor for grazing their sheep (a stint is five acres). When Willie Parker's father took up the tenancy of the farm fifty-two years ago, he signed an agreement 'to protect the feathers'.

'We try to help the keepers by telling them where the predators are,' Willie said. 'Carrion crows are enemies to us all. They take the eggs and the young grouse and they'll pick out the lambs' eyes even while they are being born. The keepers on the moor keep their numbers down for us.'

Willie keeps pure pedigree Swaledale sheep on his land, not because he thinks they are the best sheep in the world, but because he thinks they suit the type of country he farms. Everything a farmer does has a reason. Everything. Willie breeds his own replacements for the flock because those sheep know the moor and they stick to their own area. When his father took over the tenancy he bought the sheep already there. There have been sheep on that moor for hundreds of years, generation after generation.

'Some years ago,' Willie said, 'we had a shearling ram. That's a ram who's been sheared once in his life, so he was about eighteen months old when we sold him. He went to one farm for two years, then another farm for two years and then another. When he was eight years old he was bought by a farmer in this area, and after he had attended to his ewes, he walked four miles back to the part of the moor where he'd run with his mother as a lamb. Sheep are not as stupid as the cartoonists like to make out. Not at all. He came home.'

On lower land the grass grows more quickly and as soon as the ground dries up, the cows can go out. On their farm at Churchdown in Gloucestershire, Adam and Ben Pullen wait for exactly the right moment to put their dairy herd out: it varies from year to year but what they want is a perfect spring day so that after a winter spent in the sheds the cows will get the full benefit of their freedom. The Pullens' cows know very well when the time is getting near.

'They stand at the gate mooing,' Adam said. 'They can smell the grass growing.'

When the big day arrives Ben and Adam make a point of watching them.

'They go absolutely crackers,' Ben said. 'Even the old ones who haven't been able to raise more than a shuffle all winter, rush around with the rest.'

The spring grass has the maximum nutrients in it and is full of energy and protein as well as 'D' value, which Ben said stands for 'digestibility'.

'The grass is like dynamite in the spring,' he adds.

A grazing cow will eat a couple of hundred pounds of grass a day, tearing it up between her bottom row of teeth and her bare gums at the top.

'Sometimes when you watch cows grazing,' said Adam, 'you'll

see them curling their tongues round it to help them get a hold. Very short grass is no good for cows. They can't get a grip on it.'

The grass is chewed briefly then swallowed to be chewed again later.

'I suppose they spend half their time actually grazing, then some more time chewing and some more time just resting,' Ben said.

'Cows like to have a lie down about midday,' Adam said. 'Ours do, anyway.'

There has always been some confusion about whether cows lying down in a field is a sign of rain. What was Ben's theory? He flashed a foxy smile.

'It's absolutely true,' he said. 'If you see cows lying down in a field, it's either going to rain or it's not.'

Twice a day the Pullens' cows come in for milking. Once the 'D' value has gone out of the grass – by June – the cows are fed concentrates while they are being milked. The amount needed for each cow is worked out and stored in a computer and when the cows have taken their places their numbers are fed into the computer and the food arrives in the right quanitity in each stall.

'The cows' numbers are stamped on their bums,' Adam explained.

Contented cows, grazing in green fields, are a pleasing sight, although a lot of people feel more comfortable if the cows are on the other side of a hedge.

'What rubbish,' Ben exclaimed. 'Cows are the gentlest creatures alive. They wouldn't hurt anything.'

But if you walk through a field of cows, they are quite likely to stop what they're doing and come and gather round, aren't they?

'What's wrong with that?' Ben demanded. 'They're curious, cows are. There's nothing wrong with that!'

It was a sore point with him because a man had recently claimed to have been attacked by some of the Pullens' in-calf heifers.

'There was a headline in the local paper,' said Ben. 'Somthing about "Marauding Heifers". I've never heard such nonsense. He just got frit.'

Adam had been lost in thought for the last few moments.

'Cows can be cruel sometimes, though, can't they?' he said eventually.

'No,' said Ben.

'Oh, yes they can,' Adam said. 'We've a pond in Church Field and when the mother duck was leading all her little ducklings down to the water, the cows clustered round them and jumped on every one.'

'That was an accident,' Ben said hotly.

'Squashed them all flat,' said Adam, not looking at all convinced.

'A bull is a different matter,' Ben conceded. 'We had a Friesian bull here once that had been shut up for a twelvemonth, and we decided to let him out with some heifers. Adam and I were walking behind him into the field and we'd gone about 200 yards when he suddenly turned round and came straight for us. We turned and ran and when we got to the gate we jumped it because he was right behind us. Then Adam climbed up on the bars and shouted "Ya Boo" at him as he charged up . . . and the gate collapsed.'

Ben roared with laughter.

'That *was* funny,' Adam agreed, pushing his woolly hat up and scratching his head as he laughed.

E aster and the first public holiday of the year. Traditionally Good Friday was the day when farm labourers planted out their own vegetable gardens. Not through choice but because they had to: they only had two days holiday in the year, Christmas Day and Good Friday. Memories of the days when farm labourers were so badly paid that those home-grown vegetables were an essential part of their diet are still clear in the minds of the old countrymen.

'My grandfather was a waggoner,' one old man said. 'That meant he had to start work at four in the morning to get the horses ready, and he would finish at six in the evening, and then at eight o'clock he had to go back to the stables to rack up and settle the horses down for the night. One Good Friday he'd been up to see to them as usual in the morning and then he'd gone into his garden to sow his vegetables. The garden was next to the road and as he worked the farmer happened to pass by. "I say, Brown," the farmer called over the wall. "If you're looking for work, there's plenty up at the farm." '

It was probably a light-hearted remark – even an attempt at a joke – but the memory had rankled down through three generations.

'I've never forgotten that,' the old man said bitterly. 'Farm work was next to slavery. If it wasn't for Christianity, we'd never even have had Sundays off. That's one thing we have to thank them for.'

Easter weekend, weather permitting, is probably the first opportunity for people to take a look at the countryside, and immediately one of the greatest divisions of opinion between city dwellers and countrymen comes into the open. It is over the matter of dogs. The city dweller's dog is regarded as a friend, with as much right to enjoy a day out in the country as his human companions. A farmer, gamekeeper or sportsman expects his dog to earn its keep. Whether it's shepherding, or retrieving, or hunting, a country dog's life revolves round its work. Rarely on the leash, always with one eye on the boss, the country dog moves like a shadow at his master's heels. One thing you never do is to suggest to a countryman that his dog might be less than perfect. Every shepherd will tell you that his dog is the best in the county. It may not be up to competition standard, but for what he wants, 'There's no dog can beat it,' he will say with quiet pride. 'Trained her myself. She's steady.'

The keeper has very strong views on dogs.

'A dog reflects on its owner,' he said, 'and vice versa.' Some of the dogs brought to the shoots he organises do not impress him.

'They go around all day with their noses up the bitches' tails. All they can think about is getting them in the litter-way. That's no good is it?'

Farmers do not hesitate to let you know you should not let your dogs run loose where there are sheep about, especially at lambing time. 'PLEASE LEASH DOGS OR WILL BLOW HEAD OFF' was the message chalked on a stile leading into a field of sheep. That is clear enough. Farmers are legally entitled to shoot any dogs worrying sheep, but it is more difficult for the keeper, who has to patrol fields which at first sight may look empty, but which, as the year goes on, will be full of young pheasants. This is where the clashes come.

'Some of those dogs have never had anything run away from them before,' Bob Carter said. 'They've never had so much fun in their lives. There's no stopping them.'

So he puts up a sign asking people to keep their dogs under control and still he finds people with their dogs running loose in his fields.

'I go up to them and tell them I'm the keeper and do you know what they say to me?'

For a solitary man, doing a solitary job, the keeper is a great performer. When he gets wound up, he acts the story out, playing all the parts himself, and the subject of dogs certainly winds him up.

'Do you know what they say?' he repeated. 'They say: "Oh you're one of those bastards are you? You're one of those people who raise pheasants just to be shot at. That's wicked!" They don't seem to realise that being chased by a dog isn't much fun for the pheasants either.' He pulled his cap down over his eyes and brooded for a few moments. 'I put up this great big sign, and they ignore it,' he said. 'So I go up and ask them if they have trouble with their reading, and they tell me I'm being rude! Or else they tell me they didn't see the sign,' he said. 'Now I ask you. You wouldn't try that on with the police, would you? If the police pulled you up, you wouldn't say "Oh sorry, Officer, I didn't see the sign!" You'd get done for driving without due care, or being blind or something, wouldn't you?' He shook his head.

'And then they say they thought it was all right for their dogs to chase wild things and I say, "Well, I'm bloody wild now, so it had better chase me!" And *then* they say, "My brother-in-law has a farm and he doesn't mind us running our dogs there," and I say, "Well, why don't you bugger off back to your brother-in-law's then?" and then they tell me I'm being rude again.'

Bob Carter opened up his eyes wide, the picture of injured innocence, fed up with the injustice of it all.

By April the ear will have formed inside the wheat . . . quite invisible and perfectly protected, but all ready to grow, given the right amount of warmth and sunlight and rain. The solitary figure walking the fields of growing corn at this time of year will be the farmer.

'The best fertiliser is still the farmer's boot,' said Charles Amos. 'You've got to get out there and take care of the crop. Watch it all the time.'

Charles Amos farms 230 acres of grade one arable land in Kent. He is a pleasant man who looks like an advertisement for pipe tobacco. He is watching his crops for any sign of disease and explained that little patches on the leaf mean there is fungus there.

'I always need two pairs of glasses when I'm walking the crops,' another farmer said. 'One to see where I'm going and another one to look at the plants.'

If there is any infection, it is up to the farmer to decide how serious it is. Can he get away with not spraying? Would his time and money be better spent doing something else? The decision to spray has to be weighed up against the fact that any tractor moving through the crop spraying fungicides, insecticides or growth regulators is inevitably going to do some damage to the growing corn. Even using the 'tram lines' still clearly visible from when the corn was sown, the crop is bound to suffer, and yet if the right spray is not applied when it is needed, *everything* could be lost.

A cereal farmer spends a lot of time on his hands and knees looking for trouble. Apart from worrying about his wheat, Charles Amos was still waiting for the soil to warm up enough to get his potatoes in. They were late already, but you cannot plant a potato in soil that is too cold and wet. The previous year his crops had all been safely planted by this time, eyes open, growing sturdily.

'You never can tell,' Charles said, sounding remarkably calm and civilised about it all.

'By Christ it had better stop raining soon,' Peter Philpot shouted down the telephone to a farmer friend. 'It's pissing down here at the moment.'

Peter Philpot farms 7,750 acres in Essex and he, too, was still waiting to get his potatoes in.

'Farming is all a matter of timeliness,' he said. 'You wait for the right moment and then, when the ground is fit, GO MAN GO!'

Apart from potatoes and peas, Peter Philpot grows winter wheat and barley and oilseed rape and pick-your-own fruit and vegetables. Because his farm is accessible to the public, he tries to give the public what it wants. They can pick almost everything that it is possible to pick and if they do not want to do that there is a Farm Shop from which to buy and a Farm Museum to look round.

'I've diversified,' he said.

He certainly has.

'Pick-Your-Own is a gamble,' he said. 'For instance: it costs £800 per acre to establish the strawberries, and if the weather is wet when they're ready to pick, you can lose a lot of money. You have to have fine weather, and not only that, it has to be fine at week-ends when people want to come and pick them. It's worse than backing horses.'

All Peter Philpot's tractor-drivers have CB radios fitted in their cabs and there is a radio link between Peter Philpot and his foremen, wherever they are. He believes in communication.

'It's essential; it saves time,' he said, picking up the receiver in his Range Rover. 'Calling Badger, calling Badger,' he shouted into it.

Silence.

'Where the hell is he?'

We went looking for Badger (one of the foremen), screeching along the narrow concrete paths between the fields of pick-your-own. Peter Philpot's own call sign is 'Tiger'; it suits him. He is a lean, neatly dressed man about half the size his disembodied voice would lead you to expect. There were a few, damp people picking daffodils in the rain.

'Penny each,' Peter said pointing towards the daffodils. 'That's not bad, is it? We missed bloody Easter, though, they weren't out in time.'

We found Badger, surrounded by a sea of mud, discussing a new machine with the man who had just left it. Peter Philpot said that if the machine would do the job they wanted, they would have it. Driving backwards, the way he had come, very fast indeed, he told me that the public who come to pick the fruit and vegetables are a good lot on the whole.

'You get the odd rogue who tries to hide their pickings under the hedge instead of paying for them, but apart from that they're very good. Some women come out picking in high heels and mini skirts,' he said, whizzing round a corner and stopping in front of the house. 'The blokes love it. You've never seen so many big bums bending over in your life.'

He got out of the Range Rover and disappeared into the house at a run. When I found him again he was in the kitchen, talking to his broker on the telephone.

'All right, all right,' he shouted. 'I can add up. I'll get back to you later.'

The broker had been wanting to know if he was ready to make a deal on his potato crop. These were the potatoes not yet planted, and selling non-existent potatoes is another gamble; if the potatoes failed to materialise, he would have to buy in to make up the difference. Peter Philpot loves a gamble. His black eyes sparked with pleasure as he made up his mind to take a chance.

He sat down for a moment to explain why he thought farmers had been getting such a bad press.

'I don't think the public understand what we farmers have achieved,' he said. 'The Government asked us to produce more and we did. But the only way we could do that was by using modern methods. You can't work with big machines in small fields, you know. Do they really want us to go into the twenty-first century as peasant farmers? The trouble with people today is they've forgotten what it's like to be hungry. The public say they don't like it when we spray the crops, but they don't like creepy-crawlies on their cabbages either: I sometimes wonder if they know what they do want. We spread some animal manure on the fields recently – good old-fashioned farm dung – and we got letters complaining about the smell!

'People drive out here, take a look around and say, "You've ruined it!" All right, we've had to take out some hedges, but we've planted 15,000 trees in this area and nobody has even noticed them. What has your average Mr Townsfolk gone out and planted? We have actually done something. We farmers look after the countryside. Nobody else does. If we stopped growing our crops and left the land to become derelict, they wouldn't like that, would they?'

Peter Philpot said that he worked hard.

'People don't realise,' he said. 'I'm on call twenty-four hours a day, seven days a week and I enjoy every minute of it. Part of the reason is that I like the men I'm working with. They're the salt of the earth.

'People used to think of farm-workers as a lot of carrot-chewers but, believe me, they're not. They've got to have plenty going on between the ears these days. They're dealing with machinery that's worth a lot of money. A combine costs £60,000 and a pea viner costs £120,000 and we've three of those.'

But if the machines are as up-to-date and costly as anything in industry, there is one big difference between running a manufacturing plant and running a farm.

'If you were in charge of an assembly line knocking out washers or something like that,' Peter said, 'you would know, or you *should* know exactly what your product would sell for. We don't know what our costs are going to be; we don't know how much we are going to produce; and, at the end of the day, we don't know the price it will sell for.'

Peter Philpot employs two full-time fitters on the farm and three more to look after the machines in his plant hire business.

'You can only succeed if you pay attention to detail,' he said.

And what personal qualities would he say a farmer needed?

'You have to have the feel for it,' he said. 'You have to kick the dirt and know the right time to go in.'

And you have to be a keen businessman. Peter Philpot always takes advice about what to spray and when, and he gets two or three different opinions before he makes up his mind.

'I would hate to think I was being conned,' he said. 'We don't spray unless we have to. Spraying costs money.'

When he orders seed for planting from his seed merchant it is on condition that they deliver on time.

'And for every day they're late,' he said with a tight smile, 'they know I'll hold my cheque back for a month. That perks them up.'

Peter looked at his watch.

'The Farm Museum should be open,' he said, and hurtled out of the house towards the building by the side of the main road where the collection is kept.

He has poured £100,000 in this museum so far. He has bought a number of steam-driven tractors, and one of his semi-retired fore-men has the job not only of showing people round, but also of restoring the machines to their original, gleaming glory.

'A lot of farmers were just cutting them up for scrap metal,' said Peter. 'I thought they ought to be preserved. I wanted my own son and everybody else to have the chance to see things like this. I think they're important. It's part of farming history isn't it? I love farming. I know there are farmers who are a lot better than me, but I do try.' Suddenly he looked vulnerable, as if he had said too much and was regretting it. He was rescued by someone calling him to another telephone call and he was gone in a flash. The museum is a considerable achievement – a collection of farming implements which traces their development from the earliest, wooden tools to the sophisticated machines of today.

Leaving the museum, later on, it was still raining, and the concrete farmyards were deserted, but disembodied voices zapped between the tall storage buildings and the machine sheds. 'Tiger' was on the airwaves again.

While the farmers make sure that their stock have plenty to eat, the wildlife have no husbandmen to see them through a late spring. Nature does not provide; there is nothing for them to eat, particularly in harsh upland country.

Ivan Swaile was born in a cottage on the moors above Hexham in Northumbria, on land that is now deep under the waters of the Keilder reservoir. On his evening off he decided to drive up the moors and see for himself if there were any signs of spring.

'When it is very wet there are more slugs around,' he said, 'so the farmers spread slug pellets and the pellets kill the mice and the birds. Everything has its effect in the end. There was a sudden decline in the numbers of peregrine falcons and golden eagles in the fifties and an enquiry discovered that it was because the shells of the eggs the birds were laying were abnormally thin. That was due to the mercury-based seed dressings the farmers used on their fields. The birds were on the end of the food chain, but they were still affected. The barn owls have almost completely disappeared now because there is nowhere for them to nest. All the barns have either been converted into houses or they are being used for stock.

'People seem to be living today as if the end of the world was coming. They don't plan for the future. More and more people want to go shooting and fishing. They want the good life. I used to do a lot of shooting myself, but I've given it up now. Apart from the pheasants reared by the keepers, and the red grouse, what is there to shoot?

'All our wildlife is under pressure and nobody is going to do anything about it. Nobody.'

As we drove higher and higher towards the grouse moors, Ivan stopped the van to listen for the sound of snipe. At this time of year the male birds make a humming noise with their outer tail feathers as part of their mating ritual. We listened. Nothing. No snipe drumming, only a rolling, sighing silence all round.

'Wait a bit.'

We waited. And then a voice spoke from behind us in the van.

'Fish Two Three. Come in Fish Two Three.'

It was one of the under-bailiffs calling Ivan on the radio. He had found a bag and some snorkelling gear on the bank of the river.

There were footsteps leading down into the water, but none coming back.

The voice on the other end of the radio sounded urgent. Ivan smiled gently.

'Stay where you are, Steven,' he said into the microphone. 'Just stand by the bag. We'll come down. Maybe somebody's drowned. We'll see what we can fish out. Over and away.'

We turned and drove back to the river; Ivan, who is always calm, becoming even calmer.

'Talking of dead bodies,' he said, 'I am appalled at the number of dead hedgehogs I see on the roads. I drive 20,000 miles a year and I've been doing that, day and night, for thirteen years, and I've never killed a hedgehog yet. That leads me to believe that there must be a lot of people with bad eyesight driving cars.'

We arrived back to find the bailiff standing by a holdall on the river bank, exactly where he said he would be. Just at that moment two young men arrived, wet and panting. They had tried to canoe downstream and capsized. They were from the army training camp nearby and said they had just gone out on the river for something to do. End of incident. Back up to the moors.

Some of the finest grouse moors in the country are in Northumbria. The shooting rights alone can sell for something like £500,000, but the tenant farmers who keep their sheep on the moors have been encouraged by government grants to increase their flocks.

'There's nothing written down about how many animals per acre or anything like that,' Ivan said. 'You understand what I mean?'

The sheep and the grouse are competing for the same space and the same food and the increase in the number of sheep has meant a decrease in the number of grouse. Grouse cannot be reared in pens like pheasants. They pair off to nest and their staple diet is the tender shoots of new heather. All the keepers can do is to burn the heather on the moor in strips so that there is always some new growth, and to try to keep down the predators.

'After that,' Ivan said, 'you are in God's hands.'

A wet spring means that the heather will not burn. It is also disastrous for ground-nesting birds; not only the grouse, but the lapwings, curlews, larks and redshanks which nest on the moor.

'A bird can't incubate when the eggs are under water,' Ivan said. 'Some of them will have tried to produce one lot of eggs already and those will have been lost. And it's always the first clutch that's the strongest, you know.'

He suddenly pulled over to the side of the road and stopped the van. There was never such a man as Ivan Swaile for pulling up, switching off the engine and winding down the window all in a matter of seconds when there was something to see or hear.

He had stopped because there was a black grouse, sitting on the stone wall by the side of the road. Black grouse were once quite common in the northern counties of England, but in recent years their numbers in Northumbria have declined to almost nothing.

'They're the sort of bird that's not so good at rearing their young,' said Ivan. 'If they're disturbed, they don't come back to the nest. They're not so devoted.'

The grouse shot by the syndicates on the moors from the 12th August every year are normally red grouse.

'They'll shoot the black grouse if they can find them,' Ivan said. 'But I don't think they should. I think under the circumstances they should be protected.'

The bird on the wall was glossy black with white wing bars and a small tuft of red feathers on its head. As we looked more closely we could see four more of them on the grass on the other side of the wall. Ivan said they were all males, explaining that the female is dark fawn, a quite different colour. The reason all the black cocks were together, Ivan went on to explain, was because they were 'on the lek' – a dancing display performed by the males at mating time.

'When I was a boy living on the moor, we used to have to close the bedroom windows at night when the blackcocks were on the lek. They make a bubbling noise that can be heard for miles and it was so loud, we couldn't sleep.'

The grouse all flew away in silence. It was too cold for their ritual dance. The snow was still thick on the higher ground and it had snowed again only that morning.

We got out of the van and walked down a lane towards an isolated farmhouse in the distance. The great, wide silence was broken only by the sound of the wind sighing through the rushes and by the cry of lapwings. Then a flock of curlews suddenly came into sight and circled the sky away to our left.

'They'll have just arrived from the coast to nest,' Ivan said, standing still to watch them and taking a long breath. 'My, that's a good sight,' he said. 'That has refreshed me.'

Over the wall we could see two redshanks on the moor and a pair of lapwings flying together, round and round, crying their mournful cry, as haunting and forlorn as the countryside around us.

'Beautiful, yes' Ivan said, 'but they should be sitting by now. That's all wrong. One of them should be sitting tight by this time.'

Three hares were sitting further down by the stone wall. As we got nearer they crouched, ears flat, glassy-eyed, before loping off across the grass. Suddenly more lapwings flew up.

'The farmer will be coming,' Ivan said. 'They're all up.'

The farmer was hidden by the wall, but the birds had given him away.

'We'll stay and have a word with him,' Ivan said. 'We'll just have a bit crack with him.'

A few moments later the farmer's head appeared suddenly over the top of the wall.

'How do?' he said.

'How are you?' Ivan asked him.

'I'm in better fettle than the weather, or I'd be in a bloody mess, wouldn't I?' the farmer said, laughing.

'Have you seen any migratory birds yet?'

'No, not a one. I've been looking every day.'

'It's serious,' Ivan said. 'Very serious.'

They talked about the people they knew in the area, and the story of how the farmhouse in the distance had been attacked by such a huge swarm of bees a few years back that they had blacked out all the windows. A bird flew over some trees in the distance.

'What do you think that was?' Ivan said.

The farmer said it had been a pheasant and Ivan nodded. But as we walked back towards the van he said:

'That was no pheasant, but the worst thing you can do is to contradict a countryman, you know.'

The cold was keen and penetrating, but the evening sun was lighting up the green grass and the tawny brown rushes on the moor with a gentle glow that looked like warmth. There was a sense of relaxation and recreation in the air after the serious business of the day.

'This is the best time of all,' Ivan said. 'Just before dusk. So many people who want to have a look at the countryside drive out and maybe take a picnic lunch, but that's not the time to see things at their best. This is the time.'

It was true. The birds, the hares and the lambs, racing each other across the grass, all seemed to be aware that to be alive in that place at that time was something to celebrate. Like the meek they had inherited the earth.

> *Blows the wind today, and the sun and the rain are flying,*
> *Blows the wind on the moors today and now,*
> *Where about the graves of the martyrs the whaups★ are crying*
> *My heart remembers how!*
>
> (Robert Louis Stevenson)

★ Whaups – curlews.

MAY

May – the very name of the month has a kind sound to it. Not brisk like March or flirtatious like April (promising everything and then walking away, laughing), nor sombre like October. May is more of a mother figure, watching over all her new-born animals and birds, green-fingered in her country garden, decorating every corner of her house with flowers. Richard Jefferies, the nineteenth-century naturalist and writer, described the succession of flowers at this time of year:

> *The primroses last on to the celandines and cowslips, through*
> *the time of the bluebells, past the violets – one dies but*
> *passes on life to another, one sets light to the next, till the*
> *oaks and singing cuckoos call up the tall mowing grass to*
> *fringe summer.*

The flowers cover the woodland floor before the leaves come out on the trees and the canopy keeps out the sun. Everything has its time. In May the cow parsley appears from nowhere; tall and white, waving from the verges by the roadside over the whole country. As it grows the fields are hidden from view; the narrow lanes become deeper and more mysterious; and just for a while when it is first in bloom, its strange, elusive fragrance fills the air. And then suddenly, one day, standing on tip-toe, you realise that behind the frothy edges of the lapping cow parsley the corn has grown. Silently the green tide has come in, until each field of wheat and barley seems like a green inlet, filled to the brim, deep and cool.

And May is, above all, the month of leaves and blossom. The sweetest scents fill the air – and what do the farmers do in this most poetic of all the months? They cut their first crop of silage. Silage is pickled grass, well known for its disgusting smell. Ben and his brother Adam in Gloucestershire start making their silage in early May.

'Silage has revolutionised stock farming in the last twenty years,' Ben said enthusiastically. 'We take out a ten-foot mower one day and then go back twenty-four hours later with the precision chop forage harvester. . . .'

It sounded like something from the dinner-time conversation at 'Cold Comfort Farm':

'Why has not the barren field been gone over a second time with the pruning snoot?'

What is a precision forage harvester?

'It's the machine that picks up the grass and shreds it,' Ben said briskly. 'Then we bring the silage back, put in the clamps, make it airproof and cover it with something heavy.'

The strange heaps that rise up around farmhouses covered in black plastic sheeting and weighed down with old tyres are silage. If farmers run out of room in their clamps, they leave huge plastic bags of the stuff piled up in the corners of their fields. 'Wonderful stuff', according to Ben.

'It honks a bit,' a farm-worker said, 'but the animals love it.'

'What smell?' Ben said indignantly. 'Our silage doesn't smell, does it Adam?'

'I can't smell anything,' said Adam, sniffing the air like a bloodhound.

To the untrained nose silage does smell, but if you get close enough to it, it smells quite sweet.

Venning Davey is a tenant of the Duchy of Cornwall and farms 250 acres in Blisland, near Bodmin. He too, keeps a dairy herd, and grass management is a serious business for him. He replaces the grass on his farm every five years, ploughing up and reseeding some fields every year. Every one of his fields, surrounded by their towering Cornish turf hedges, is as individual to him as their names – Outer Andrew and Big Andrew, Inner Gum and Higher Down, Yonder Park and Penny Quindles – and he worries constantly about the quality of grass they are producing.

'People think of farmers as insensitive brutes who go around raping the countryside for their own advantage,' he said.

He shook his head. He is a quiet, thoughtful man, deeply

concerned that people should understand what he does and the reasoning behind it. Tall and slim, wearing overalls and a cap that has become moulded to the shape of his head, he is a man used to keeping his own counsel. Out in the fields he covers the ground with a long unhurried stride, while his eyes are always searching the distance, checking his stock, his land and the sky.

Venning Davey spends from April to September alternately looking up at the sky and ringing the meteorological office to find out what the weather is going to do next. There is an old saying: 'In the winter it rains everywhere, in summer where God chooses.' God should really have a word with Venning Davey before he chooses to let it rain in Blisland in the last week of May. Venning likes to cut his first crop of silage on 24th or 25th May.

'And that is not just a date plucked out of the air,' he said. 'That is the date when the grass will be at its best, and just before it goes to head. In this part of the country if you started making your silage on May 20th, you would have no stem on it at all, which is good, and the 'D' value would be high, but you would not get much of a crop. If you left it until 2nd June you would get more tonnage but the 'D' level would have dropped.'

A few, short days can make an enormous difference. A cow eating silage made in May would maintain itself and give two gallons of milk a day, while a cow eating silage made in June would give no milk whatsoever.

'The cows are the ones to tell you,' said Venning. 'But its not so simple as that,' he added with a smile.

It never is quite so simple with farming. Once the grass has been cut, it is left to wilt for twenty-four hours, and for that there must be sunshine. If the weather is wet and misty the farmer will have to consider using an additive to prevent the silage going mouldy.

'That is a big decision,' Venning said. 'The salesmen say: 'Use our additives and sleep easy in your bed.' But the additives cost something like £2,000. The question is, if you know your overdraft at the bank has just gone up by £2,000, do you sleep any easier?'

The bacterial action of the additives solves the problem of grass that is too lush and green when it is put into the silage clamps.

'If you end up with a foul-smelling gigantic muck heap instead of silage, that is when you wish to hell you had spent the £2,000,' Venning said. 'But by then it is too late.'

Farmers are notorious for complaining about the weather, but there can be few ways of life where the profit on a whole year's hard work can be wiped out by one devastating downpour. For dairy farmers whose main crop is grass, the weather can not only ruin their summer, but will leave them without sufficient food for their stock the following winter.

'Then you are in real difficulties,' Venning said. 'All you can do is buy in more food or sell off some of your stock. But whatever you do, you will never get out financially sound. If the weather has affected you, it will have had the same effect on all the farms in your area so the price of food goes up and the price you get for your stock goes down.'

It is not a bit of good trilling on about the merry, merry month of May to a farmer when it is raining on silage grass.

Spring is in the orchards and the blossom is out; cathedral-like aisles of trees spreading away into the distance, clouded in white; a hovering mass of blossom, and of bees. Hundreds of hives of bees are brought to the orchard in May to pollinate the trees, and the whole operation is orchestrated by Bill Flynn, beemaster, from his home in Dartford in Kent. Bill Flynn is Secretary of the Bee Farmers Association, and from January onwards he is busy marrying up fruit farmers who know they will want bees in their trees with bee farmers who can supply them. The Bee Farmers Association has four hundred and sixty members, each of whom has forty hives or more.

The need for bees has been growing steadily over the last twenty years because, according to Bill Flynn, insecticides and the destruction of the hedgerows have resulted in a loss of 99 per cent of the natural pollinating insects.

Kent is one of the main fruit producing areas in England and the biggest fruit farms there will need as many as seven hundred hives of bees for their orchards. In May a hive might contain something like 20,000 bees, but their numbers are growing all the time, because from February onwards the Queen Bee will be laying two thousand eggs a day.

'Yes, two thousand,' Leo Hiam, a bee-keeper from Gloucester said, smiling. 'We want some chickens like that, don't we?'

The fruit farmer waits until about 20 per cent of the blossom is out on the trees and then rings up his bee-keeper and asks him to bring the bees in. The bee-keeper has to move quickly. A five-ton truck will hold a hundred hives, but who drives the truck? The bee-keeper does.

'Have you ever tried asking someone to drive a hundred hives full of bees for you?' Leo Hiam asked.

If all the blossom comes out at once and all the farmers want their bees at the same time, the bee-keepers spend night after night driving up and down the motorways with their loads. They cannot set off until late evening because they have to wait for the bees to stop flying before they can load up the hives.

'You can't whistle the bees in when you want them. You just have to be patient,' Leo said.

Either that or they set off at three o'clock in the morning when the bees are asleep and hope to get to the orchards by dawn. Once the sun is up the bees will want to fly, and even though the hives are closed up for the journey, the bees are quite likely to find a way out. Leo remembers stopping at a motorway café just before dawn. When he went back to his truck he found it would not start.

'The manager of the café came running out in a terrible state. He said, "What are you going to do with all those bees?" "I don't know," I told him. "But if the sun comes up you are going to be in a lot of trouble." '

Bill Flynn's bees got out once when he was driving them to Faversham.

'They were in thick, black clusters all over my arms and there wasn't a thing I could do about it,' he said. 'A bee farmer earns his money, I can tell you.'

The bee-keepers like to place their hives in the middle of the orchards where there is no chance of their bees being distracted from their task by a field of oilseed rape or by bluebells in a nearby wood. The difficulty is that most people who work in the orchards would prefer the hives to be as far away as possible.

'It's surprising to me that so many people born and brought up in the country are afraid of bees,' Bill said.

Perhaps country people know that May and June are the swarming months; but if the bee-keeper has done his job properly a swarm should not happen. And if the bees should swarm?

'Don't worry,' said Leo. 'They shouldn't hurt you. They've just gorged themselves on as much honey as they can eat – enough to last them until they find a new home – so they tend to be at their best natured in a swarm. If they are not, God help you when you've got them in the hive.'

If a hive does become over-populated and gets 'swarm fever', the queen bee will lay eggs in special cells which are then filled up with Royal Jelly by the worker bees. The queen and the flying bees will then leave the hive to look for a new home and seventeen days later the eggs in the special cells will start hatching out. What happens next is still something of a mystery. The experts think that the first queen to hatch out of the special cells begins to 'pipe' and the rest of the still-unhatched queens respond with the same high-pitched noise. Having identified her rivals, the new queen then makes her way along the cells filled with Royal Jelly and stings all the other would-be queens to death.

'Queen bees certainly do pipe,' Bill Flynn, the beemaster, said. 'I've had hatching queens in the house and I've heard them. It's quite a loud noise.'

A queen bee will never sting a human being, but that does not mean she has no sting.

'When we are artificially inseminating a queen, we have to lift up the sting flap to insert the syringe,' Bill Flynn said.

You need good eyesight to artificially inseminate a bee. Not many people try. Most bee-keepers select a queen for breeding purposes and then let nature take its course.

'Some people breed for temperament,' Leo Hiam said, 'some breed for bees less inclined to swarm, but personally I try to breed bees that collect the most honey.'

When the queen first hatches out she is a 'virgin queen' until, seven days later, she takes her 'Maiden Flight' and meets a drone:

'And that,' said Leo Hiam, trying not to laugh, 'is her lot. That has to last her a lifetime.'

Having returned from her 'Maiden Flight' a queen bee will never leave the hive again, unless she leads a swarm.

Leo Hiam is not interested in collecting strange swarms: as he said, 'You never know where they've been, do you?' But if he has to go and pick up a swarm of his own bees he takes them back to the hive on a cloth.

'Then I put a bit of wood up from the ground to the entrance of the hive, shake the bees out of the cloth and they all march up the drawbridge into the hive like little soldiers. The only trouble is that if I've missed the queen and the bees find she's not in the hive, they all come marching out again.'

The bee-keepers are paid by the fruit farmers for the work their bees do because there is not much honey in it for the bees or their owners. So, after about four weeks in the orchards, it is back on the motorways again . . . back home for the serious business of making honey in June and July.

In May the keeper becomes a blur on the landscape. Once the pheasants' eggs begin to hatch the chicks are put into the brooder houses which are weatherproof and heated by calor gas. The keeper is still feeding the adult birds in the laying pens, turning the eggs in the incubator three times a day, and visiting the brooder houses up to seven times a day to make sure the chicks are all right.

'If it's a warm day and the gas lamps are turned up too high, the chicks get themselves roasted,' he said. 'On the other hand if it turns cold they will catch a chill. Believe me, if the wind blows the wrong way those birds take it into their heads to die.'

It does seem slightly incongruous that a hefty, healthy young man should be spending his days fussing over little birds no bigger than a ping-pong ball, but he is not only their nursemaid, he is also their minder.

In his book *The Open Air*, published in 1885, Richard Jefferies wrote:

> *A naturalist has recorded that in a district he visited, the nightingales were always shot by the keepers and their eggs smashed, because the singing of these birds at night disturbed the repose of the pheasants!*

A farmer told me that as far as he knew the keepers' rule was: 'If it has a hooked beak, shoot it.'

'People will always say that if anything looks sideways at a pheasant the gamekeeper will have it,' the keeper said. 'That's not true.'

What about those dead crows or magpies you used to see strung up in fields? Wasn't that the keepers' way of warning predators off?

'How could it?' the keeper said, glaring at me over his moustache.

'I thought it was meant to act as an example; to discourage the others.'

'You're talking about "vermin lines",' the keeper said. 'The old boys used to get paid a bonus for any vermin they killed. That's why they strung them up like that. We don't do that anymore here.'

The natural enemies of the pheasants' eggs and chicks – and of the pheasants themselves – are stoats, weasels, foxes, magpies, crows, mink in some areas and feral cats.

'Our job is to maintain the natural balance in favour of the pheasant,' Bob Carter said.

The balance is all important. Any changes in the way things are done in the countryside have far-reaching and often unexpected consequences. If pheasant shooting was abolished the face of the countryside would change because there would be no reason to maintain the 'warm woods' full of undergrowth which acts as cover for the birds, and if there were no keepers the pheasants would soon become an endangered species . . . not only pheasants, but a wide variety of wild birds whose only lifeline in a severe winter is the food scattered by the keeper in the woods for his birds. There is a direct relationship between conservation and sport, which has to be acknowledged by anyone with the welfare of the countryside at heart.

'Take foxes for example,' Bob said. 'Foxes kill for pleasure. Nine out of ten times they don't eat what they kill.'

Foxes come out at dusk and move into the fields to hunt.

'They like to keep to cover as much as possible,' the keeper went on, 'especially the older ones who stick to the side of the hedges as if they were attached by a piece of string. If you know the area well, you can anticipate exactly which way they will go.'

Bob Carter organises two or three fox shoots early in the year to keep their numbers down. He invites a few trusted colleagues to join him.

'I only invite people who can be relied on to shoot foxes and not each other,' he said, grinning.

Later in the year, when the young pheasants have been released into the woods, he has to keep a look-out for any fox that might be threatening them. How does he know a fox has been there? Bob bent down and ran his hand across the thick covering of acorn husks on the ground.

'Because it hasn't rained recently,' he said, 'these are all dry on top, but if you turn one over you will see that underneath it is much darker with the damp. If a fox had walked across here, he would have disturbed the ground very slightly, so one or two of these would be lying damp side up. That's how you know.'

Setting out after a fox, single-handed, is where the keeper's knowledge of the area and of the fox's movements becomes invaluable.

'And if all else fails,' the keeper said, 'I can bring him to me by making a noise like a rabbit caught in a trap. That fetches him. He wants to know what's going on.'

Challenged to imitate a dying rabbit, the keeper put his hands to his mouth and produced a series of inhuman screaming, squealing noises. Good enough to fool a fox? The keeper said so. It would have to be good, as the fox's reputation for cunning is no myth. One of the best examples is quoted by Ian Niall in his book *Fresh Fields*. A farmer had been losing his chickens to the foxes, so he set a trap and the next morning was delighted to find a dead fox in it. The farmer explained what happened next:

> *He wass dead. I put my foot on the trap an' lifted him out. New-dead, he wass, and warm. I laid him on the bank and set the spring of the trap again. When I looked up he wass off! Off like the very wind, he wass. Never looked back! My gun was round the corner. Foxin' he wass! Foxin'! Next time I take a dead fox out of a trap I'm going to kill him just to make sure.*

Ian Niall also describes his own meeting with a fox:

> *He stood not twenty feet away and looked at me. 'So this is the old red fox,' I thought. It was enough to gladden my heart, and still is, the memory of the fox, standing there at the edge of the thicket, looking back at me with one paw raised, and his sharp face full of the devil.*

'I would hate to see the last fox dead,' Bob Carter said. 'It would be disappointing.'

War breaks out in the hop gardens in May. It is an annual battle between the farmer and a very unusual insect that nature seems to have designed specifically to be the perfect pest. Charles Amos keeps 40 acres of hops on his arable farm in Kent and he is an expert on these aphids, which are a type of greenfly.

'The first migration of winged aphids comes over from the orchards in May and, from then on, they will come over in wave after wave for the next two and a half months, right up to the end of July or the beginning of August.'

Rather like a mini Battle of Britain in fact. Charles Amos first scrambles his tractors in early May to put down a soil drench. The idea is that this will make its way from the soil into the leaves of the hop plants so that any aphid that sticks its little needle mouth into the leaf will get a dose of insecticide. The aphids counter-attack by breeding at a startling rate. Having wintered, wingless, in the fruit trees, they produce a winged generation in May which flies to the hops and this generation then gives birth to successive wingless generations. In order to save time, the aphids give birth to live young instead of laying eggs, so the new generation are all ready to go and will be producing young themselves within ten days.

Constant watching and constant spraying are the only answer. Charles Amos keeps up a regular patrol of his hop fields, looking under the leaves for the visitors.

'If you did nothing they could strip the hops bare, and if they were still there at harvest time they would turn the hops black, because the honeydew produced by the aphids attracts sooty mould. Aphids gorge themselves on plant sap – they eat so much of it that it actually trickles out onto their two little horns at the back. It's pure carbohydrate and the ants love it. In fact ants will keep aphids in a nest and milk them for their honeydew.'

The small groups of people you see on their knees in hop gardens in May are not members of the farmer's family praying that the aphids will give them a miss for once, but casual workers brought in to twiddle the hops.

Hop training is a fiddly business. Each hop plant has to be encouraged to wind itself round the strings which run from the ground to the top of the frame. Hops are notorious for having the strongest likes and dislikes. They like to be twisted round the string in a clockwise direction, otherwise by the next morning they will all have unwound themselves again. The hops look like neat little strawberry plants when they start growing. They clutch at the strings which reach from a corkscrew peg next to them right up to the frame fourteen or sixteen feet above. Looking down at the modest little plants it seems a tall order for them to grow so high so fast.

'Oh, they'll get there all right,' said Charles. 'They'll be up there by Midsummer's Day, They always are.'

In May, as the fresh, green leaves come out on the trees, the woods beckon:

> *In the warm wood now*
> *Between grief and grief*
> *Blithe is every bough*
> *And every leaf;*
>
> *Though death's behind me,*
> *Death not far before,*
> *Undying beauty*
> *Is at my door.*

(Elizabeth Daryush, *Spring*)

Every wood has its own character. Every wood looks different, sounds different and smells different. While a wood of broad-leaved trees is full of birdsong and movement, a conifer wood is darker and more silent. It is part of John Hammond's work, as woodman/warden for the National Trust, to survey and assess woodland. He needs to know exactly what is there, not only the trees, but the birds, insects and animals.

'A wood is not just a lot of trees standing about for people to admire,' he said. 'A wood is a dynamic entity.'

To see as much as possible you have to approach a wood in the right way. The first reaction to an intruder is usually a series of alarm calls from invisible birds somewhere overhead and a round of applause from a wood-pigeon, taking off in a hurry and clapping its wings over its back as a warning that you are coming.

The game is up before you have started. How does John Hammond do it?

'The most critical time is when you first enter a wood,' he said. 'Think about it like going into a room where you don't want to be seen. So, you don't choose the most obvious opening but look for the "back door" where you can slide in unobserved. However cautiously you move, if you listen carefully, you will be horrified by the noise you are making; you can hear this infuriating din going on and it will only stop when you stop.'

The more often you stop, the better, because the more you will see and hear. You need plenty of time to walk through a wood if you want to see more than the trees and possibly the rear end of a disappearing rabbit.

'If you stop and look around you, you can take in the detail,' John said. 'You might catch a glimpse of a crossbill or a tree-creeper, or see a spider swinging down from a branch with its cluster of eggs, or notice an owl pellet at your feet, full of fur and minute bones from its last meal. You would have missed all that while you were on the move.'

Countrymen have the ability to look in two places at once. While they are taking stock of what is immediately around them, they are also watching to see what is happening in the distance.

'Where you stop is important, too ,' John said. 'The human form is one of the most easily recognisable shapes there is. A rabbit, a pheasant or a deer will freeze and their shape is lost because they instinctively use cover to break up the line – the form – of their bodies. That is all camouflage is.'

To camouflage the human shape you need somewhere with enough cover to change your outline, but that does not mean you have to be completely hidden. Both John Hammond and the keeper have stood within a few feet of unwelcome visitors and have been passed unnoticed, although they were perfectly visible. It is movement that catches the eye.

John went on to explain that you can use the same camouflage method to get near animals, providing the wind is not carrying your scent in their direction. Deer and rabbits will start when they recognise your presence, but they do not always run away immediately: if they are not sure they will stop and watch, all ready to go, but waiting to see if the threat is real.

'If you can keep absolutely still until they have satisfied themselves there is no danger, they will begin feeding again and might even move nearer to you,' said John, 'but that "safety period" of theirs can seem a very long time to a human being. It's like a battle of wills.'

Bob Carter had been talking about the same thing but in particular about the skill and patience involved in stalking fallow deer.

'It's the waiting that makes it so worthwhile,' he said. 'If you don't spend an hour in one spot, you're wasting your time. Even an hour is not very long. What's an hour? But keeping still for that long is painful. Have you ever tried keeping still for even ten minutes?' he said. 'It hurts.'

John Hammond was about to make an assessment of a wood for the National Trust. It was just the trees he was interested in this time, so he could walk and talk as he went. The wood was Petts Wood, only twelve and a half miles from London, owned in the seventeenth century by Phineas Pett who, although he used the timber for his shipbuilding yards in Deptford, did have the sense to replant what he cut down – much to the satisfaction of the keeper at Petts Wood, Tony Hall. Tony has the responsibility of the day-to-day care of this green oasis in the Green Belt. He is a man who normally spends his time alone. Long-haired and gentle, he speaks very quietly, as if he were talking to himself, when he speaks at all.

'This is very much an amenity area as opposed to a commercial woodland,' said John Hammond, reverting to official woodman-speak because he was on duty. 'The value of the timber here is not the standpoint from which the Management Plan will be drawn up.'

Tony Hall said nothing.

'This wood is unique,' John went on, lacing up his heavy boots and trying to stop Tony Hall's tame squirrel from running up his legs. 'It's unique because it is so near the city. It's right next to a built-up area, but still it is rich in content. It gets a lot of pressure but it still has a diversity of habitat and wildlife, and it has a nice, natural feel about it.'

By this time the squirrel was sitting on top of his hat.

'Get this thing off me, will you,' he said, laughing and trying not to move. 'You know I think these things are vermin. What would my colleagues say if they could see me now?'

The squirrel raced down his arm and bit him on the finger.

'It *is* a wild animal,' Tony said apologetically and coaxed it away with a nut.

John handed me a map to hold while he got out his handkerchief to use as a bandage. What exactly was he planning to do in the wood, besides bleed?

'I am trying first of all to get an overall impression,' he said stoically. John and Tony Hall consulted the map, which had been drawn up some years ago by the National Trust and which divided the wood into compartments, each with a different mixture of trees or ground cover separated by paths, ditches and bridleways. We started with compartment 25 because that, as it turned out, was where we were standing. The ground underfoot was soft and springy from generations of fallen leaves. All around the songs of invisible birds merged into a background of sound; as we stopped to listen, they were identified by Tony as those of the robin, wren, blackbird, thrush, dunnock and chiff-chaff. There was a scuttling noise behind us. It was the squirrel hurrying to catch up. Tony took it back to its tree again. Meanwhile John Hammond was making notes of the trees around him.

'Some good standard oaks and a fair bit of alder,' he said as Tony Hall came back.

'They used to make gunpowder out of alder trees, you know,' Tony Hall said. 'They made it into charcoal first, then gunpowder.'

'Where's all this sycamore coming from?' John asked.

'The surrounding properties, I think,' Tony answered. 'When the ground is wet I pull the young saplings out. I've cleared some of it.'

'Yes, but come autumn and winter you're going to have millions more. They're very invasive trees, sycamores,' John continued. 'You could get rid of them with chemicals, you know.'

'I'm not having chemicals in my wood,' Tony Hall said firmly. 'I'll carry on pulling them out.'

We stopped to admire a particularly beautiful oak tree and Tony pointed out a hole in one of the branches where a nuthatch was nesting. Inside the hole was a ring of lighter material.

'They line the hole with mud so that it's just big enough for them to get in and out but too small for any other bird,' he explained.

A tall conifer had a row of holes going up the trunk making it look like an outsize flute.

'Woodpeckers?' John Hammond asked.

'They were woodpecker nests,' Tony said, 'but they've been taken over by starlings now. Once a starling has used a nest the woodpeckers won't go near it again. They must make an awful mess or something.'

John Hammond found an old poplar tree and did not like the look of it.

'They're a bit unpredictable as they get older,' he said. 'They're very susceptible to fungal attack. You can't see anything from the outside but then, one day, they can just snap like a carrot. In my opinion they are ugly things anyway.'

Tony Hall said he liked poplars because even on the stillest summer day there was always some movement in the leaves.

John Hammond and Tony Hall agreed that a little discreet tree planting would be a good idea. Some of the oak trees were a couple of hundred years old, and, as John Hammond commented, they 'can't last for ever' and natural regeneration cannot be relied upon. The old trees will not be felled because they make valuable nesting sites, but in the open spaces, among the brambles, new trees will be planted . . . planted very unobtrusively because some people cannot be trusted to leave a young tree to grow in peace. Members of the public, walking their dogs, passed by without giving the two men a second glance, completely unaware of the amount of thought and care involved in maintaining a woodland – with a 'nice, natural feel about it' – for them to enjoy.

While John Hammond was busy with his notes, for the Management Plan, Tony Hall explained how much he enjoyed his solitary life.

'How can you ever feel alone with all this going on around you,' he said, 'under your feet and in front of your eyes and over your head? The woods tell you things all the time. I could just stay in one spot for hours and there would always be something of interest going on. But you have to be prepared to become part of it, to feel it, smell it and get it under your fingernails. Trees are endlessly fascinating. Look at that Scots pine . . . the bark. If you asked people what colour that was, they'd probably say brown. That's not brown is it? Look at all those shades and variations. Each tree is an individual in its own right. All together they make up a wood and, if you don't interfere with it, there's a harmony there that man could never achieve. People tend to think in "tidy" or "straight lines" and that's all wrong.

'You can stand in a wood and your ears will tell you if anything is amiss. You hear a sudden lull in the birdsong or the wrens start making that chacking noise, or the blackbirds and starlings give their alarm call. That could mean there's a fox about, or a crow, or just that they've come across an owl roosting near their nest.

'I can even hear the sun on the trees sometimes. The sun warms up the bark and it expands and when you get a lot of trees together, they make music. Some people think I'm a bit eccentric when I tell them that. But it's true: you can hear it if you listen.'

JUNE

What is a summer day? . . . .
It is a continent, from pole to pole
(From mist-white dawn to evening) all the way
A paradise, wherein the scenes unroll
Of warmth, of wonderment too sweet to say.

(Elizabeth Daryush)

June puts to shame those who doubted her. All through the previous months there have been misgivings. 'Not many swifts about,' someone says; 'The blackthorn is late,' someone else remarks; and then, one day, June takes her place in the countryside – unruffled, fragrant, a shimmering enchantment – and from the softly rounded shapes of the fresh-leaved trees, the hushed coo-ing voices of the pigeons reprove us: 'I *told* you, didn't I? I *told* you.'

The combined scents of wild roses and newly cut grass are the essence of June.

In the past June was the time when every able-bodied man in the community would turn out and help with the haymaking because without hay there would be no winter food for stock. In 1796 Ann Hughes, a farmer's wife in Herefordshire, kept a diary (published in 1964 as *The Diary of a Farmer's Wife*). For 'June ye 5' she wrote:

> *We have got the two bottom grounds of grass cut, and John do think all be cut down this week. They all hard at it from cum day light till it be dark. The men do drink much cyder, and eat great lumps of bread and cheese, but all do work with a will. . . . June ye 10 – This be the first chance I have had to write in my book for nigh a week, we being*

89

*verrie busy with the hay, which did make in fine fettel, and
we able to stack it verrie quick. . . .*

So much depended on getting the hay cut, dried, stacked and
thatched over to keep out the rain before the weather broke that,
according to Richard Jefferies: 'signs and tokens of birds and plants
and the set of the wind at particular times were regarded as veritable
oracles to be inquired into not without fear and trembling.' There
was no note so hated by the haymakers as that of the thrush,
because, supposedly, they did not sing in dry sunshine.

It is to be hoped that Ann Hughes's husband John finished his
haymaking 'verrie quick' because on 'June ye 16' she wrote:

*It did thunder much to-day, the lightenen did strike the elm
tree by the big gaite, and did kill one of Johns cows, I fere
he will be rathe for dayes, I must feed him well and so
hummer him. Men be just like childer and as much trubble
in many wayes, but John be a good husban and I would not
like to lose him, he bein just a gret babbie for sure. . . .*

On a blazing hot day in June, I found Harry, the forester, taking an
early lunch, stretched out under a tree with his flask of tea,
reminiscing about the days when he used to help with the haymaking. In his childhood the hay was still stacked in the fields, and when
Harry was ten years old he was a 'stomper'. His job was to stand on
top of the haystack and stamp the loose hay down as it was pitch-
forked up into a space half way up the stack, known as the 'Lovers'
Hole'.

Why was it called the 'Lovers' Hole', I wanted to know.

'Use your sense,' Harry said, getting back to his story. 'It was hot
work, haymaking,' he said, 'but the thing about those old boys was
you never saw them stripped off the way you see people today.
They'd be wearing their combinations, a flannel shirt and a waist-
coat on top of that. They used to say, "What keeps the cold out,
keeps the heat out." I don't know how they stuck it,' Harry said and
laughed, and poured himself out another mug of tea. 'They were
good old boys,' he went on. 'Real, dry sense of humour they had. I
remember one day we was haying, and one of the old boys had just

90

lifted up a big load of hay on his pitchfork when two ladies from the big house happened to pass by. 'How much does that weigh, my man?" one of them asked him. "Seven hundredweight, ma'am," he said, quick as a flash and absolutely straight-faced.'

On a modern farm, the making of silage is the key to successful stock feeding through the winter. Haymaking is a much more low-key affair, as I discovered when I visited Chris and his father David Parker on their farm on the borders of Northamptonshire and Leicestershire. They had cut the hay in one field and it was drying out, ready to be baled up the next day or the day after. Chris Parker explained that the hay was useful because it was the most convenient way to feed sheep in winter and because the Parkers need hay for their horses, adding that they 'just make it for fun, really'.

'What happens if it rains?' I asked.

'It won't rain,' Chris Parker said.

He is an athletic-looking young man, skin deeply tanned by the sun, sleeves rolled up, very much the outdoor type, while his father looks as if he spends his life in an office. On the 900 acres they farm they keep sheep and grow wheat but their main interest is in their fat cattle, some of which are raised intensively on silage while others are bought in the spring, grazed on the rich pasture land through the summer and sold in autumn. The summer grazing of beef cattle is the long-standing pattern of farming in the area.

'Traditionally if you lived in this part of the country, you were a grazier,' David Parker said. 'Up to the last war there wasn't a ploughed field within twenty miles of here. This is ancient pasture land. Something very special because of its richness and the variety of grasses that grow here.'

We stood, leaning over a gate and watching the Parkers' glossy, fat cattle wandering among the buttercups in the shimmering heat of a perfect June day. Thick, green hedges divided the fields, and groups of trees dotted the landscape. This is hunting country. In the eighteenth century the first Hunt Club was founded at Melton Mowbray and, as a direct result of the popularity of riding to hounds, the landscape of the East Midlands was created and a way of life for the local landowners was established which suited them perfectly – spending their summers grazing their cattle and their winters hunting and shooting.

'What you did *not* do in this area was keep dairy cows,' David Parker said. 'You were not considered to be a farmer at all if you milked cows, because by doing that you were binding yourself to the cow. That was, and still is, a "non" thing to do.'

He was very firm about that.

'I can remember when my grandfather owned this farm in the 1930s,' he said. 'Times were hard . . . so hard that we were selling rabbits to make ends meet. One day my grandfather found my father measuring up the barn and he asked him what he was doing. My father said he was working out how many milking cows the barn would take. My grandfather told him that if he brought a cow onto the farm, he would be out. And that was the end of that. Anyone forced to turn over to milk was assumed to be no good at wheeling and dealing in the cattle market, you see.'

'Buying a beast cheap and selling it dear is a peculiar skill,' Chris Parker said. 'It's not something you could sit down and learn in a classroom.' Chris looked sideways at his father: 'I suppose I learned from watching him.'

David Parker's mild-mannered appearance could be dangerously deceptive in an auction ring.

'When I go to market I'm looking for something that somebody else has made a mess of,' he said. 'I know I've got this marvellous grass and I know if I buy a beast with a bit of age, something between fifteen and eighteen months old, I can make a job of it.'

The Parkers buy cattle in the spring that have been kept through the winter on just enough food to keep them ticking over but no more.

'Once they are turned out, they should make up for lost time,' Chris said. 'The skill is to be able to spot the ones that will put on that burst of compensatory growth once they get here.'

'Cattle do best when they lie warm at night,' his father said. 'We all like sunny summer days, but warm nights make all the difference.'

'There's a lot of psychology involved in buying cattle,' Chris said. 'If you go and tell some farmers you like the look of their cattle, they'll be so pleased they will practically give them to you, whereas others will decide that if you think they are that good, they might as well stick the price up.'

'It's the farmers who look thick and aren't that you have got to look out for,' said David. 'The ones that move around a bit quick you *know* are on the ball. Be wary of the sleepy-looking ones, I always say, and anyone who smokes a pipe.'

Wheeling and dealing in the market-place is obviously something David Parker has got down to a fine art.

'Selling is a different matter,' he explained. 'You have to decide what that beast is worth and *make it* make it. You have to keep up the emotional temperature round the auction ring. If you can get somebody really wound up, they will probably pay more than they intended to. You'd be a fool if you let an animal go for less than it was worth.'

Turning away from the gate, David Parker indicated the surrounding countryside with a sweep of his hand.

'The lives of all the people who live in this area follow a set pattern,' he said. 'Our work and our leisure pursuits have always been interwoven and they always will be. It is all part of the country scene and the countryside is as it is because of these things.' He looked me straight in the eye: 'I don't see what makes anybody think it should be any different.'

In June the ear emerges on the wheat. Since late March or early April the ear has been fully formed but hidden, cocooned in a green sleeve in the centre of the plant; but once it emerges in June the grain-filling process can begin.

A field of wheat changes in appearance every time you look at it. It is one colour in sunshine, another when the sky is overcast and at night it gleams like silver in the dark. Best of all are the days when the clouds race across the sun and send shadows sweeping over the fields in waves of gold and grey.

A field of wheat is an ordered multitude of growth, a million million plants in which each ear will hold about the same number of grains and each of those grains is complete in itself.

In *Field and Hedgerow* Richard Jefferies describes these separate entities:

> *If you look at a grain of wheat you will see that it seems*
> *folded up; it has crossed its arms and rolled itself up in a*
> *cloak, a fold of which forms a groove, and so gone to sleep.*
> *It is narrow at the top, where the head would be, and broad*
> *across the shoulders, and narrow again towards the feet, a*
> *tiny man or woman has wrapped itself round with a garment*
> *and settled to slumber.*

While the grains sleep in the sun under the singing larks (the collective noun for larks is an 'exaltation'), the farmers have little time to exalt. June is the time when they have to make up their minds about next year's crops. They have to work out their rotation, and order next year's seed. What crop? What variety? Which field? If the corn looks like doing well this year, what should be sown next? A break crop, perhaps.

A break crop gives the land a rest from corn, restores essential chemicals to the soil and prevents a build-up of disease. A break crop can be anything from beans to peas, oilseed rape, maize, or potatoes. Farmers are beginning to experiment with new crops like evening primroses, borage, flax or maize – anything that might find a market. They all have their own ideas about what they like to grow and what suits their land best.

'I don't like beans,' Alan Riddlestone said. 'Beans are a lazy man's break crop. All you have to do is to sit on your arse on a combine.'

While the farmer works out his next move, he has to consider the individual characteristics of each field. Copse Ground and Pig's Green, The Follies and Razor Meadow. No Gain – that speaks for itself, doesn't it? – 'That's a hard old field.' The decision about what to grow and where is no easy one. As one of the contributors to Gail Duff's book *Country Wisdom* says: 'A farmer should live as though he were going to die tomorrow; but he should farm as though he were going to live forever.'

During June there is a gradual transformation among the sheep. All the matronly ewes suddenly strip off their woollen coats and emerge pinkish-white and bulging in all the wrong places. The annual sheep shearing has begun.

Some farmers still shear their own flocks, but these days with fewer farm workers employed, more and more sheep-owners are calling in contractors to do the job for them. Roly Ellis runs a sheep contracting business from his farm in Berkshire. During the shearing season he has nine separate gangs working for him, all recruited from New Zealand where Roly spent some time before setting up in business in this country. His gangs move round from farm to farm, shearing something like 120,000 sheep in six or seven weeks.

To organise all this, Roly Ellis spends a lot of time on the telephone in his office, keeping tremendously calm, even when the weather upsets all his carefully worked out arrangements. The problem is that you cannot shear a wet sheep.

'Wet wool snags on the combs and cutters, and wet and grease give the shearers grease boils on their legs,' he explained.

Roly Ellis is a tall, commanding figure, but he needs all the discipline and organising ability he picked up during his army days to keep his customers satisfied and his shearing gangs fully operational at this time of year. He tries to work things out so that the sheep to be sheared outside are done in fine weather and those that can be sheared under cover are done when it is raining, but, not surprisingly, this does not always work out.

Although there have been improvements in the last fifteen years, Roly Ellis still considers that, on the whole, 'sheep are still the "forgotten" animals in this country, the poor relations of the stock-keeping world.' Whereas the hill farmers on the whole are very proud of their stock, Roly Ellis feels that people in the lowlands tend to think of sheep as just another commodity on the farm.

One of the problems for Roly Ellis is that as the weather warms up it brings out the grease on the sheep which moves through the new white growth of fleece right through to the weathered tips of the wool.

' "Weathered" is the word,' he said. 'If you tell a farmer his sheep look dirty, he'll never speak to you again.'

Once the grease comes out, the fleece 'rises' and the sheep are ready to shear. The farmers take one look at their flocks and rush for the telephone to call in the shearing gangs. All of them at once.

'It gets pretty hectic,' Roly Ellis said, running his hand over his sleek, dark hair and smiling bravely.

'The grease makes an awful mess of your trousers,' an old shepherd said, 'but by the time you've finished shearing, your hands aren't half soft and lovely. The grease is lanolin.'

The worst thing that can happen to one of Roly Ellis's shearing gangs is to arrive at a farm and find that nothing has been prepared for them and the sheep are still scattered round the surrounding fields. Ideally they like the sheep to have been rounded up and housed the night before so that they are sure to be dry, and because it is better if a sheep has been starved immediately prior to shearing. This is because a full-stomached sheep can injure its intestines when it is upside down at a shearer's feet.

'They gas up,' the old shepherd had said, darkly. 'Sheep are full of gas, you know.'

Roly Ellis answered the telephone again. It was another farmer in urgent need of a shearing gang. Roly Ellis told him he could do a rush job for him as long as he had the farmer's assurance that his shearers would not find 'an old granny flock' waiting for them.

'Wrinkly sheep take longer to shear,' he explained as he put the 'phone down.

The whole of Roly Ellis's life revolves round sheep, whether it is buying or selling them, clipping or dipping them or advising on sheep management.

'Keeping sheep is a state of mind,' he said. 'If you get on with them, you can usually beat them at their own game.'

He decided to visit one of his gangs who were working at a farm nearby. As he drove to the farm he explained that first impressions can tell you a lot.

'If you find an immaculately tidy farmyard, you can be pretty sure the sheep are going to be in good condition,' he said. 'Running a farm is like running anything else. Those who are organised do well and those who live in chaos go down the drain.'

The farm we arrived at was definitely not going 'down the drain'. The shearers were working in a modern outbuilding, open at one end and fenced off for the day by metal interlocking barriers.

Each shearing gang consists of two men and a girl. The male shearers had been paired together by Roly Ellis because they both worked at about the same pace. After learning the job in New Zealand they had both been to 'Shearing School' over there to perfect their technique.

'You have to shear a couple of thousand sheep before you become really skilled,' Roly said, 'but of course there are plenty of sheep out there to practise on.'

As we walked towards the metal barriers, one ewe, just finished off by one of the shearers, scrambled to her feet, walked halfway across the front of the barn and then suddenly sprang high into the air in a weirdly silent, private moment of glee, before trotting briskly away. As they say in Yorkshire of anyone putting on an unexpected burst of speed – 'She went like a clipped 'un.'

All the lambs had been separated for the day, to be reunited with their mothers later.

'It takes them a while to get mothered up,' one sheep farmer said. 'The ewes know their own lambs all right, but the lambs are not so sure at all, not even when they've had a good sniff. I suppose the ewes smell different when they've been clipped.'

As we got closer to the scene of action, the air was thick with the smell of sheep, lanolin and sweat. As Roly put it: 'Clipping is a juicy business.' The two New Zealanders were standing side by side in front of a pen of sheep. They were thin, sinewy men, wearing ragged vests, greasy trousers and flat, felt slippers. As they finished with one sheep they went straight into the pen for the next one, picking it up from behind by the front legs and sliding it along the ground on its bottom. Work starts as soon as the shearer is back in position, with the sheep sitting at his feet, staring up into his face, apparently completely relaxed.

'Half the art,' said Roly, 'is to know how to hold the sheep so that it is fairly comfortable and doesn't want to wriggle. Until you have mastered that, they will be squirming all over the place. When I

97

started I even had them getting away from me and running all over the paddock half-shorn.'

The method of shearing the New Zealanders were using was invented by a countryman of their own called Godfrey Bowen in the 1950s. The Bowen method meant that not only does the fleece come off in one piece, but by rolling the sheep round as they work, the shearers can keep going in the same direction all the time, which makes a quicker and, some say, a better job of it. Each sheep takes between forty-five seconds and two minutes to shear. The idea is to finish the job with as few 'blows', or strokes, of the 'headpiece' as possible. The 'headpiece' is the set of electric clippers attached by a long wire to an overhead power-point, something like the arrangement of a dentist's drill.

'That's the motor,' one of the shearers (called Hughie) said. 'We're the engines.' Without stopping work he went on. 'The faster you can go the easier it gets. As you become more experienced you don't have to bend over quite so much. At first you're holding the sheep with one hand all the time because you haven't the confidence just to grip it between your legs. I can remember the first time I tried shearing. There were six sheep and the farmer sheared the first one to show me how it was done and then went off and left me to it. When he came back an hour later, I'd just managed to shear my second sheep. I'd been bent double, fighting those animals every minute of the time and I was absolutely stuffed!'

Hughie looked up, grinning all over his thin, freckly face.

As the clippers whirred up towards the neck of the sheep he was holding, he said:

'You're scared stiff of cutting them at first, too. There are a few veins you have to watch out for. . . .'

'The jugular vein,' Roly Ellis said.

'That's right,' Hughie said cheerfully. 'I've never actually cut any throats myself, but I had one sheep the other day which was absolutely covered in shit so you couldn't see what was what. The farmer is supposed to tell you if there is anything special to look out for, you know, but this farmer hadn't said anything to me. I didn't know that that particular sheep had two tails.' Hughie looked up and grinned again. 'It's only got one tail now,' he said, 'be all right for next time.'

Hughie's latest client was almost done. The girl member of the gang was crouching at his feet, ready to pull away the fleece, roll it up and tie it in a neat bundle. The ewe scrambled away and performed its private, ritual dance, but Hughie was not looking. He was already in the pen getting another sheep out. He and his partner had been working for six hours and had sheared five hundred sheep, but there were still plenty more to go before the end of the day.

One of the outstanding features of the landscape from the York-shire Dales to the northern borders of England is the dry stone walls built to divide up the land in areas where the climate is too harsh for hedges to grow. The walls enclose the grazing and winter fodder fields next to the farmhouses – the 'in-by land' – and then snake away over the fells; thousands of miles of stone walls, all constructed without the use of mortar and relying on the skilful placing of stone on stone for their durability and their strength.

The walls were first constructed in the eighteenth and early nineteenth centuries and they were made to last. Every year, however, there are repair jobs to be done on them, where small sections of the wall have collapsed because the rainwater trapped inside them during the winter creates movement among the stones as it freezes, thaws and freezes again; or where the hardy local sheep have knocked a piece of wall out by constantly trying to jump over it. Being able to do these repair jobs, or 'gapping' as it is known locally, is skilled work.

Harry Waller is a dry stone waller who works within a fifty-mile radius from Hesket Newmarket in the north of the Lake District. His name fits his job as neatly as a well-placed stone. He repairs walls for farmers and landowners all year round as long as the weather is fit. Snow or frost are the only things that will stop him. When he was young he knew a dry stone waller called Wilf Kipling.

'He was a character, was Wilf,' Harry Waller said. 'When it was pouring down with rain or something of that nature; when the weather was atrocious, he used to say, 'We'll pick an inside job today,' and then he'd put a sack round his shoulders and go out and do some walling.'

Harry Waller first started dry stone walling twenty-six years ago. He is a slim man who looks a bit like a character from Dickens with hair curling round the back and sides of his head, short side-whiskers, and very direct blue eyes. Walling is a solitary job, especially up on the high fells and, with plenty of time to think, Harry Waller is a man of firm opinions who is ready to challenge anyone's point of view if he doesn't agree with them, no matter who they are. He has the tenancy of a small sheep farm at the back of Skiddaw with 'going on for 200 ewes'. Going on for?

'You'll never get a sheep farmer to give you a definite number,' he said. 'They'll always say "round about" so many, because ten to one if they tell you the correct number, there will be one or two dead the next time they go out. There's nothing a sheep likes better than dying on you unexpectedly. At lambing time you might go out for a last look round just as it's getting dark, and when you get back the wife says: "Everything all right?" and you say, "Champion. Grand." And, by God, you go out next morning and everything is wrong. You can never take anything for granted.'

Harry Waller shepherds with a dog. His sheepdog, Ben, is getting old, and when I met him, he had just bought a new one, bred from good stock, which he was going to train himself. He brought her out and she bounced up and down in a sitting position at his feet, gazing up into his face, desperate to please.

'She's as soft as a boiled turnip,' he said, smiling at her, 'but she'll make a dog.' He had called her Floss. 'All working dogs have short names,' he said. 'They have to be short and sharp, you know, Drift, Nip, Fleet, that sort of thing. Just the one syllable.'

The view from his farm was breathtaking. In Elizabethan times they discovered more varieties of minerals in the northern range of Skiddaw than anywhere else in the country. Queen Elizabeth I said that the area was 'worth all England else', and Harry Waller would go along with that, minerals or no minerals.

He put the dog away and set off to do some walling. On the way we passed some posts set into a marshy bit of land by the road.

'The National Park people found some orchids there,' he said, 'and because I was secretary of the Caldbeck Commons Committee, they rang me up and asked me if they could fence off the area. I said that they could if they liked, but had they considered that by doing that they would be changing the environment. A fence would stop the sheep from eating the grass, do you see, and it's obvious the sheep weren't eating the orchids or they wouldn't be there, would they? Another thing is that a fence excites people's curiosity, doesn't it? That made them think.'

Further on we passed a car parked in a remote spot with some people with binoculars sitting on the bonnet. They were local worthies, taking their turn on a twenty-four-hour watch over a peregrine falcon's nest.

'The birds have been nesting in that same spot for fourteen years,' Harry Waller commented drily. 'I hope those people don't frighten them away.'

The wall he had come to repair was near Blencathra, or Saddleback Mountain. At first sight the collapsed section of the wall looked a very nasty mess; just a heap of stones of all sizes lying on the ground without any visible form or structure about it. The first job you do when you are 'gapping', he explained, was to move most of the loose stones, or 'clemmies', out of the way. He picked them up, one by one, and threw them just behind him and gradually, as the majority of them were cleared, the big foundation stones became visible and there were the beginnings of a wall. Having made sure that the foundation stones were firm and straight, he filled in the middle of the wall with smaller stones, or 'heartings', and then he was ready to begin building. There was a rhythm about his movements and an economy of effort that is the sign of a true craftsman. If he was bending down removing stones from the broken wall, he stayed in the same position, throwing the smaller stones through his legs and shifting the bigger ones to one side or another. If he was rebuilding he would pick a stone from the pile behind him, stand up with it and place it on the wall in a space that seemed to have been made for it.

'This is where you have to watch out for the quarry mouse,' he said. 'If a dry stone waller gets his finger trapped under a stone he says he's been bitten by the quarry mouse. It usually happens with one of the first stones you put on, or else one of the last.'

When Harry Waller turned to select a stone, he would pick it up, turn back, toss it between his hands and then place it on the wall, sometimes turning it over and trying it on the other side before he was satisfied. The most unlikely shapes seemed to fit somehow.

'There's a place for every stone,' he said and he picked up another one. 'How many ways could this go? Six ways maybe, but there is only one right way.'

Harry Waller learned a lot of his skill from a man called Wilfred Emmett, a dry stone waller who used to live in the Yorkshire Dales – where Harry was born.

'He was a small man, Mr Emmett,' Harry said. 'Five foot five, no more, but he was a man and a half. He always used to say to me, "Never handle the same stone twice." You see, as a beginner to the job you pick up a stone and you're not quite sure, so you put it down and try another one, but if you go on like that, think of the weight you're lifting all the time. "Never handle the same stone twice," he said, so I said to him, "Well, what *do* you do if the stone you've picked up just won't fit?" and he said, "You throw the bugger away."'

An experienced dry stone waller can look at a wall, get a picture in his mind of the shape of stone he needs next, turn round and pick up the stone he wants without wasting a moment.

'You have to photograph it in your mind,' Harry Waller said. 'If you went through the whole pile every time, it would take you an eternity.'

He placed another stone on the wall that was growing under his hands. The stone rocked a bit because it was uneven underneath. He selected a small, flat triangular stone and pinned the bigger stone with that so it was absolutely firm.

'It's all right, is that,' he said. 'People come along sometimes when I'm walling and they say, "Wouldn't it be nicer if all the stones were straight?" Or they want to know why the walls themselves aren't straight. I say to them, "Turn round and look at the view. How many straight lines can you see?" They follow the contours of the land, do the walls.'

Behind him as he worked was Souther Fell. It is said that a ghostly troop of horsemen have been seen sweeping down the fell towards the valley at various times. Phantom soldiers maybe, or ghostly border raiders. But no ghostly horsemen were visible that day, only the shadow of clouds chasing down the slopes, followed by dense mists that brought sudden squalls of rain with them. The appearance of the mountain ranges changed every moment with the changing sky, and sometimes, as Harry Waller worked, a cuckoo would call from the distant fell, with a sound that was as sweet as a nut.

'People ask me if I paint,' Harry said. 'I don't need to paint. That's the painting out there. It's been partly painted by the people who have lived and worked here for generations, but they've painted it with their skills, not with a brush.'

He filled in the centre of the wall with some more small stones and then chose a longer one to place sideways across the wall.

'End in: end out,' he said. 'If you put this one lengthways, the weight of the stones above it would spew it out.'

'Through' stones are often used to strengthen the wall, but they can only be used if they are there to use. If there has been a quarry in the area there are more likely to be bigger, flatter stones available but a dry stone waller has to use whatever is to hand. Because he is a contractor, working over a wide area, Harry Waller is used to working with every kind of stone, from pebbles from the becks in the valleys, to sandstone, green slate, Skiddaw slate, gabro, lime-stone or granite. Skiddaw has been found to be composed of one of the oldest rocks in the world.

'This is "forever" stone,' Harry Waller said, heaving a small boulder into place. 'These stones represent time. These days we seem to want to scrap everything that's old, don't we? But a thing only becomes old because it's been tried and found successful. Am I right?'

The irony is that although the walls are essential as boundaries and as shelter for stock high up on the windswept fells, no-one actually wants to claim ownership of them.

'If there's a wall on your land that belongs to a neighbouring farmer and part of it comes down,' Harry explained, 'you "single it up" which means just putting a piece of wire across it or something to stop the stock getting through. If you do a proper job on it, you're virtually claiming that wall as your own. That's not the law, but it's the tradition round here. I met a man once who had just bought a house in the area and there was a paddock next to the house which bordered onto the farmer's land. The new owner said to me: "I bought this paddock and the farmer was generous. He said he would give me the wall with it. Wasn't that kind of him?" This man was over the moon because the farmer had given him the wall.' Harry laughed. 'Believe me,' he said. 'If a farmer can give you a wall, he will.'

The gap was nearly repaired. As Harry Waller cautiously moved some stones around in the standing wall on either side, he was listening hard. The top stones were precariously balanced.

'You have to use your ears,' he explained. 'Before they come down, you can hear them start to shunt, so you know when to get out of the way.'

Out of the chaos had come a wall, a forever wall that would not only outlast Harry Waller and the people who owned the land, but which looked as if it had stood there for generations, with the lichens, algae and mosses that had grown on the stones all put back in place facing outwards.

'I've looked at a great many paintings of landscapes,' Harry said. 'Some of them by very well-known artists. But, do you know, there's very few of them can paint a wall. They miss the detail, and the variety. They just can't capture it, somehow. That's surprising isn't it?'

When he is repairing a wall there is no way that Harry Waller can tell if that particular piece of wall was built by one man, or if one section was built by one workman and another by a different man. The workmanship is always the same because there is only one way of building a wall with the stones available. There is no way of knowing who did the original work as no names of wallers are written down and no record of their achievements has been kept.

'People are always asking me if I find many valuable things in the bottom of these walls,' Harry Waller said. 'What a question! These men had nothing. The only things I have ever found are old clog irons, broken clay pipes and very old cough medicine bottles for the "consumption" as they used to call it. My idea of dry stone walls is that they are a monument to the men who made them. They are monuments to cheap labour are these walls.'

JULY

Summer has reached her peak. The grasses have produced their seeds, the corn has changed colour in the fields and the first soft fruits are ready for harvest. The year is perfectly poised between growth and ripeness, and nature seems to hold her breath because any shifting of that balance will bring with it the first hint of decline and decay.

In the cottage gardens the rich colours of the flowers glow in the strong summer sun, the hollyhocks stretch their thin necks against the walls and, in the wood, the wild foxgloves climb flower by flower to their full height, measuring, with delicate precision, the year's meridian.

At Peter Philpot's farm in Essex, everyone is on red alert. The pea harvest has begun and it is GO MAN GO time. The pea viners, monster machines, twenty feet long and twelve feet high move out into the fields, clearing an acre (or three tons of peas) in an hour, slashing open the pods and separating the peas for the next stage of their journey to the canning or freezing plants. At the farm there is a steady hum of activity while men and peas move purposefully in all directions. In the office I found Philip Blair, third-in-command pea-wise, in charge of operations. He explained that the pea harvest lasts for thirty-five days and that the overriding priority is to get the peas to the factory as quickly as possible so that they will arrive at their best and sweetest.

'We are the sandwich,' Philip Blair said. 'On one side is the crop and on the other the factory demanding a through-put of peas. Peter Philpot rings the factory and asks them when they can take delivery and whether they say three o'clock in the afternoon or three o'clock in the morning, we make sure that a twenty-ton load of peas leaves here to arrive at the factory at exactly the right time. We have people working right round the clock.'

As Peter Philpot said, the secret of success is timing, absolutely spot-on timing.

Before they are harvested, the peas are tested for tenderness. A pea-sampler goes out at four o'clock every morning and gathers a few samples from the fields due to be cut that day. Back at the farm the samples are put into a tenderometer.

'It is very difficult to get an empirical or objective measure of quality with peas,' Philip Blair said, taking his glasses off and putting them on again.

We stared into the tenderometer, an arrangement of closely set blades looking rather like an egg slicer. When the peas are put in the blades sheer through them and the measure of force required is recorded on a dial. All being well with the reading, the pea viners will be given the all-clear to move out into the fields.

'We take the viners to the crop,' Philip Blair said, 'not the other way round. Pea vining is something that is not open to every farmer. The fact that it is done here is because of the unique character of Peter Philpot, who gets out and gets things done.'

Pea viners cost £120,000 each and Peter Philpot has three of them.

The peas shelled by the viners are either taken straight from the fields to the factories, or, if they need to be cleaned and chilled for the plants waiting to can or freeze them they are brought back to the farm. Huge high-lift trucks bring them back and tip them into an undulating sea of peas from which they move up into the cleaning and cooling plant. The water that washes over them foams and swirls and overflows as the peas move through the tanks. The floor is littered with peas that have bounced clear and the air is full of cool splashes and a refreshing pea-green smell. At the end of the cleaning process, Philip Blair explained, the peas are plunged into a tank of fresh water at a temperature just above freezing, and from there they are 'blasted straight up into the air, through the roof and out of the building'. That must be a sight. Unfortunately it all happens inside a pipe. Outside the pea shed, the pipe full of peas levels out and runs across to where the lorries wait for their cargoes, and down come the peas, water taken out, in an endless green cascade.

Behind the farm, in the fields of Pick Your Own, the strawberries were ripe and people were busy picking, bent double like coolies in a rice field, watched over by John Atkins, the Horticulture Manager, who was sitting in his Land Rover, smoking a pipe. The gooseberries were already ripe and the raspberries and currants would be ready within days and then all the vegetables would take the season through until October. Most of Peter Philpot's customers appreciate the chance to come and select their own fruit and vegetables, fresh from the earth, but, according to John Atkins, there are some who would obviously feel more at home with a tin or a packet.

'One woman came into the shop recently,' he said, 'and she must have been thirty-five years old. She'd been and picked herself the most manky-looking cabbage you've ever seen in your life, so I told her I would go and get her a decent one. I don't like people going away with inferior stuff. It reflects badly on the farm. So I got her a good one and she thanked me and explained that she hadn't really understood how to pick a cabbage, and then when she got to the till I heard her asking the girl how to cook it. I couldn't believe my ears.'

Within a couple of weeks, while the pea harvest is still in full swing, the oilseed rape will be ready to cut and then the combines will be moving into the cornfields.

'Then we really get busy,' Philip Blair said.

The first combines you see in the fields in July will be cutting the winter barley – the barley sown at the end of the previous summer. Mike Chandler, who farms in Dorset, goes into the fields and looks to see if the individual heads are ripe.

'I can look across a field from a distance and say it will be ready soon,' he said, 'but you need to be a bit more exact than that. Barley that is ready for harvest is "necked over"; before that it is swan necked and the whiskers are white. Ripe barley has hard seeds, so hard that you can just about crack them with your teeth – if you've got good teeth.'

Like all farmers, Mike Chandler uses a moisture meter to test the crop before he cuts it. Anything over a 15 per cent moisture content means that the grain will have to be dried after harvesting, but grain drying is an expensive business.

'If you have masses of combine strength and a good drier you can afford to go in early,' Mike Chandler said.

But for the average farmer it is a question of waiting until the moisture content is right. Charles Amos in Kent has to be strict with himself when he goes out to measure the moisture content of his crops:

'You're itching to get going, you see,' he said, 'so you tend to pick the driest-looking ears for testing. It's a terrible temptation because you want to get on with it. I suppose that's only human nature isn't it?'

Sitting about and waiting for the right moisture content or the weather to clear up must be horribly frustrating. The trouble with barley is that it will start to shed its seeds virtually as soon as it is ripe, so a great deal depends on the weather.

'It's the nature of the plant to shed its seeds,' Charles Amos said. 'After all, as far as nature is concerned, that is the only reason for the plant's existence. You can stand in a field of barley and hear the grains dropping out of the ears.'

They make a ticking noise. Ticking like an unexploded bomb.

'The secret is to work *with* the weather,' Charles Amos said. 'Never, never decide that tomorrow will do. It won't. It will be raining tomorrow.'

Before harvesting, those farmers unlucky enough to have wild oats growing among their crops will be out 'hand rogueing' them, literally pulling them out of the ground by hand. Wild oats are spread by birds or they can lurk in the ground and pop up unexpectedly in the middle of a field of wheat or barley.

'Wild oats are a pest,' Charles Amos said, 'and they are fiendishly well designed for the job. Their seeds have little spikes on them which bend when it is wet and straighten out in dry weather, so they can actually move themselves along the ground, like a caterpillar, until they find a convenient crack to grow in. Another infuriating thing about wild oats,' said Charles, warming to his theme, 'is that they ripen before the rest of the crop, so if you don't pull them out, all their seeds will have dropped by the time you go in with the combine and by the next year, you'll have a lot more of them.'

Wild oats may not be popular with farmers, but they look very attractive, standing tall among the corn and waving graciously at you as you pass.

By early July the cherries will be hanging in heavy clusters from the trees, ready for picking any day now. In Kent, Harry the forester was standing in his wood-yard admiring a bin full of wooden posts that he was soaking with creosote. He called me over as I passed and nodded his head towards the distance:

'Hear that noise?' he said.

Very faintly in the distance there was an unearthly wailing sound. What is it?

'That's old Robinson in his cherry orchard,' Harry said. 'He's too tight to spend money on bird scarers, so he's out there screaming at the buggers. He's at it from morning till night. He'll do himself an injury if he's not careful.' Harry laughed as the lone voice rose and fell in the distance.

Birds are a major problem for cherry growers. In spring the bullfinches attack the buds on the trees and can strip a branch in seconds. Nobody is quite sure why these birds should be so destructive. They are probably searching for insects, but one fruit grower suggested that this behaviour may be part of their mating ritual.

'If that is the case,' one farmer said sourly, 'they must be having one hell of a time.'

Next come the pigeons who eat the cherries while they are still green and then, once the fruit ripens, all the other birds arrive to enjoy the feast. Not very surprising when you think about it. The colour of ripe cherries was designed by nature to attract the birds, so that in exchange for a good meal the birds would distribute their seeds. Fruit growers are now developing smaller cherry trees because they believe that if they could cover the entire orchard with nets and keep the birds off they would increase their crop by at least 25 per cent. The towering old standard cherry trees are rarely seen these days, but even half standard trees grow to something like twenty feet and the cherry pickers on their graceful, curving ladders are the élite of all fruit pickers. The local housewives who work in the orchards in July say the cherry season is something special.

'When you're up a tree, alone with your thoughts, there's an air about it,' one of them told me. 'Once people get used to the ladders, you can't keep them away.'

At a cherry orchard near Teynham in Kent, known locally as Mother Geer's orchard, the cherry foreman, Brian Austen, strolled around the trees while the picking went on overhead. He had just taken on a couple of new pickers.

'You can tell them a mile off,' he said. 'They're the ones with their backsides sticking out.' He laughed. 'They're frightened to let go of the ladder, you see. As a matter of fact that is the most dangerous position you can get yourself into up a ladder, but never mind, they'll learn.'

Nobody was screaming at the birds at Mother Geer's, but they have tried everything else to keep them away: motor-bikes, people firing guns and waving football rattles and cannons going off from every corner of the orchard. Brian Austen said that personally he thought cannons were a waste of time and that people did not like them either – 'It gets them fed up'. The cannons are powered by gas and set to trigger themselves off at regular intervals.

'If you hear one go off, you've usually got about five minutes before it goes off again,' said Brian, 'or you should have. It doesn't always work out quite like that. Some of the cannons make wailing noises before they explode, and with some,' he said, 'you hear a noise like air escaping from a balloon and then, WHOOMPH!'

'WHOOMPH!' went a cannon, right on cue.

'It's not that bad, is it?' Brian asked, laughing, as he bent down to help pick up my belongings. The birds had taken no notice whatsoever of the noise.

'The blackbirds are not so bad,' Brian said. 'They just come along, take a cherry and fly off. But the starlings . . . they come in flocks and when they land on a tree they just seem to have to slash at everything within reach.'

So how does Brian Austen 'bird mind' the starlings?

'Shoot 'em,' he said. Now that he mentioned it, I could see that there were quite a few ex-starlings scattered over the grass.

Even if the cherry growers do succeed in producing trees small enough to net over, that will not solve the problem of rain damage. Once the cherries are ripe, they need to be picked as quickly as possible before the rain ruins them. It had rained heavily the previous night and Brian Austen reached up and picked a cherry from the tree above him.

'It's splat,' he said, pointing to a gash down the side of the fruit. 'Cracked with the rain.'

A good cherry picker will balance on the ladder and use both hands for picking.

'Yes, they fall off occasionally,' Brian Austen said. 'The theory is, that if you feel yourself falling, you should hang on to the ladder because it is bound to catch on a branch somewhere before you hit the ground. What I always tell my pickers,' he continued, 'is that if they start falling, they should make sure to pick the cherries from the middle of the tree on the way down. It saves time.' Nice man.

Twenty years ago when huge areas of Kent were given over to cherry orchards, the best pickers of all were the travellers. They arrived in force at the end of June, set up camp round the orchards, raced their trotting horses up and down the narrow lanes and won all the competitions for cherry picking.

'We used to have a lot of travellers here in the days when we were picking 3,000 trays of cherries a day,' Brian said. 'We'd draw lots for the trees at four o'clock in the morning. We marked all the trees with chalk and if No. 2 tree was a poor one, No. 2 tree inevitably went to the person who had stayed in bed and missed the draw. It was no use arguing about it. The others would swear that was how it came out.'

Today at Mother Geer's, only one family of travellers still come regularly for the picking. Brian took me across the orchard to meet them. Old Isaac, young Isaac, Aaron and Caleb and their wives and children. Old Isaac was just about to climb a ladder, a basket called a 'kepsie' strapped to his back to hold the cherries. A kepsie holds 12 pounds of cherries or one trayful. Old Isaac said that he probably picked about twenty trays a day, but that they did not start all that early in the morning, not until something like seven o'clock, he thought.

'I always put a stone in my mouth when I'm picking,' he said. 'It stops you eating the cherries, you see. If once you start eating them, you can't stop.' Old Isaac's voice was gentle. 'Cherry picking is the best time of year for us,' he said. 'Oh yes, this is the best time of all.'

Even in the country, people who can afford to stand out against the pressures of modern life, are rare. In Dyfed in West Wales I came across a man who prefers to stick to his own way of doing things. Tom Williams has lived in the same cottage for most of his sixty-eight years. Perched on top of a hill, the cottage turns its solid stone back to the road and looks out over a gentle, green valley, where Tom Williams's four cows and twenty-two sheep graze over his 55 acres of grassland. With so much land for so few animals, grass management takes care of itself. Tom Williams uses no fertilisers, nor does he own a tractor, and the cottage has no electricity or running water, but Tom Williams has life worked out to a nicety.

I found him one evening in the cowshed, doing the milking by hand. The scene inside the shed was in complete contrast to the stark, concrete brutality of a modern milking parlour. Four sleek, well-rounded cows were standing quietly in their stalls, while above their heads, on the wooden partition, sat a row of cats, watching carefully as Tom Williams, sitting on a low stool beside one of the cows, drew off the milk into a bucket. In the dim light one pure white cat shone out like a splash of white paint. There were six more cats on the floor, sitting round an empty shallow tray, and another on the window-sill next to an empty saucer. Tom Williams's first language is Welsh, but he politely switched to English to explain his method of working.

'The cats are waiting for the milk,' he explained, looking up and smiling as he worked. 'I always give them a bit from each cow as I milk it, yes, yes.' Tom has fifteen cats. . . . He did not mean to have so many.

'But they go off and have their kittens in the bales and by the time I see them they have their eyes open and you can't drown them then, can you?' he said.
Tom Williams has an answer for everything. The cows were standing quietly, chewing their cud while they were being milked with nothing whatever to keep them in their places if they wanted to move away.

'No, I don't tie them up,' he said. 'If I had a string round their necks I would only have to go to each one and undo it when I wanted them to go out, wouldn't I?'

He breeds all his own cows and he explained that he 'brought them up' to behave themselves. Pointing to the youngest one, six-year-old Blackie, he said:

'At first she wanted to run about and go out and see what was there, but I have made her stand still now while I am milking her.'

When Tom Williams had finished milking, he stood up with the bucket, full to the brim with fresh, foaming, warm milk and walked over to pour some into the cats' tray and some into the saucer on the windowsill. The cat on the sill had hers separately 'because she's the queen', Tom Williams explained.

No milk from the cows ever leaves the farm. It is all used to feed the calves produced by the cows every spring. Although milking was over, the cows stood motionless in their stalls until Tom tapped the one nearest to the open door with his stick and told it to 'go along'. The cow backed out of the stall, turned carefully in the confined space and walked out of the door, followed by the others, each in turn. Tom opened the top of the stable door at the other end of the cowshed and we stood looking down on the shining backs of the cows as they moved down the yard in single file and out towards their field. Tom made no effort to follow them. There was no need.

'Four cows are quite enough for me,' he said, 'because in midsummer on the full milk, you have a lot of milk then and there's a lot of milking to do. Some people tell me that I should get a little milking machine, but then I would only have to wash it out when I finished, and in the time it would take me to do that, I could have milked another cow, couldn't I?' He stood with his arms folded, smiling triumphantly at this argument. 'Besides, I like to do it this way,' he went on. And then he played his trump card: 'After all it's a sitting-down job, isn't it?' he said, laughing and hugging himself with delight.

The most noticeable thing about the cowshed once the cows had left, was how clean the floor was, and Tom assured me that they very seldom made a mess while they were there – 'Very, very seldom'. As he shut the top of the stable door I noticed for the first time that on the shelf above there was a row of hens and a cockerel standing so still that they looked like ornaments on a mantelpiece. They were settling down there for the night, Tom Williams said.

'Yes, yes, they insist on sleeping in here.' He picked up the bucket of milk and moved towards the door. 'I have to try to feed the calves while the milk is still warm,' he said. 'If the milk gets cold they are very cross about it.'

In another part of the long, low white-painted building that ran from the road down through the farmyard, Tom keeps his sheep-dog. He opened a door and showed me an unfriendly looking collie who barked furiously.

'She's very vicious,' he said, raising his voice above the din. 'I don't know quite why that is, but people tell me that she's a one-man dog, you see, so I suppose that is the reason for it.'

He shut the door again and went further along to the end of the building where the calves were kept.

The sheep were all out in the fields with the ram. With such a small flock, Tom Williams explained, it was not worth the bother of separating the ram, so he stayed with the ewes all the year round. That means that the lambs arrive any time from January onwards. But for Tom Williams there is no rush to catch the market at its peak. When the last lamb is ready to be sold, he will send them all together to his regular buyer, and, once a year, in autumn, he will go to Tregaron market with his calves.

Tom Williams's contentment with the smooth-running of his life is reflected in his healthy, rosy complexion and his unlined, smiling face. He does not receive many visitors at his farm, but as he walked me courteously to the gate, he told me about the day an unwary Jehovah's Witness had decided to call on him unannounced. His voice fluted with laughter as he described how he had got the best of all her arguments until she was left speechless.

'Very rude she was, anyway,' he said. 'The first thing she said was that there was muck in the yard. "Who asked you to come?" I said. I thought she was very rude. If you go to a person's house you say "Good Morning" and you might say "It's a fine day", but you don't start a conversation by making comments about the muck in the yard, do you?'

The river Itchen in Hampshire is an intimate little river, winding through tall banks of reeds and flowers, between shady overhanging trees and through ancient water-meadows, but it shares with its sister river, the Test, a world-wide reputation among salmon and trout fishermen.

One of the water keepers on the Itchen is Dick Houghton, a tall, well-built man with very blue eyes and a comfortable Hampshire burr to his voice. His stretch of river runs for three and a half miles, which gives him seven miles of riverbank to look after as well as the job of keeping down the ribbon weed which grows in the river. Dick Houghton cuts out the weed with a twenty-four-foot pole topped by a cutting knife shaped like a scythe, but he concentrates all the hard work into early mornings or late evenings so that nothing interferes with the fishing during the day. As far as the fishermen can see, Dick Houghton's job involves nothing more strenuous than strolling along the banks, smiling and serene, a walking encyclopaedia of fishing lore to be consulted whenever they feel in need of advice.

'A lot of people say they would like my job,' he said, 'but between you and me I think it would kill them in the first week.'

Dick Houghton has turned his stretch of river into a little wildlife haven. He makes it his business to know what flowers grow on the banks, as well as recording all the different birds, butterflies and damsel flies that dart and hover around the deep, quiet water.

The fishing rights to the river are sold per season or half-season and anyone new to the river has to pass Dick Houghton's scrutiny before they are accepted. All the water keepers in the area get together once a year to compare notes, and if any fisherman has blotted his copybook anywhere in the county, his name goes down in Dick Houghton's little black book and there is no fishing on the Itchen for him.

'You can always tell a new boy,' Dick Houghton said, 'but I don't mind. I've taught hundreds of people to fish. I enjoy it. The thrill they get when they catch their first fish is a joy for me, too.'

However, some of the people who turn up on the doorstep of his cottage do seem to him to have overdone it with their tackle.

'They open the boot of the car and it's like a fishing shop in there. I've always said that fishing tackle manufacturers catch more people than their products ever catch fish. Some of these modern fishing rods can cost anything from £300 to £400 . . . or you can get one for £20 which does exactly the same thing. . . .' Dick Houghton spread out his hands, shrugged his shoulders and laughed.

From Dick's point of view there are three sorts of people who fish the Itchen.

'You get the sort of person who just *has* to have a fish to take home. I call them fishmongers – all they are interested in is catching a fish no matter what and no matter how. Then there are the businessmen who come to the river to get away from the telephone and who want to sit beside the river where they are within nature and if they catch a fish, that's a bonus; and then there are the people who come for a day out and fish hard because they love fishing.'

We walked along the bank beside the river. Brilliant blue damsel flies flitted between the reeds, and butterflies sunned themselves on the flowers and swifts scythed through the air overhead, while a tufted duck guided her six babies gently across the river and a water vole swam unhurriedly into the bank.

'When you're fishing, nature comes to you,' Dick said. 'That's the best thing about it. You sit quietly and you see much more than you ever would if you went looking for it. That is if you are observant – not everyone is.'

There was a fisherman on the opposite bank. No need to ask if he had caught anything: fishermen have very expressive faces. Dick stopped and the man called over to him.

'In my personal opinion there is nothing in here!' he said. Then, obviously thinking he had better not upset the water keeper, he added hurriedly: 'Not really . . . only joking. Usual fisherman's excuse.'

'Maybe the fish are a bit dour after all this hot weather.' Dick said to cheer the man up and advised him to try a bit further down-stream.

The fisherman had been trying for salmon with a prawn for bait. He set off obediently in the direction Dick was pointing with his prawn still dangling disconsolately from the end of his line.

'I must smell or something,' he called back as he plodded away.

The idea of using prawns, or dyed shrimps as salmon bait originates from the fact that when salmon are feeding in the arctic they feed on arctic krill, which are red.

'People also use flies for salmon, which are beautifully tied feathers but don't really represent anything,' Dick said. 'The belief is that in their early stages the salmon feed on flies, so when they see a fly fished by a fisherman, the instinct comes back and they take it – that's the idea anyway. Or you can use worms, a variety of spinners or plugs.'

The flaw in all these carefully worked-out theories, is that when salmon come from the sea into the rivers, they are coming to spawn and at that stage of their lives, they do not feed at all.

'I've cleaned plenty of salmon in my time and I've never found any evidence that they feed,' Dick said.

So, if they are not feeding why should they take a bait at all?

'When a salmon comes into the river, it takes up a lie,' Dick said. 'I've watched them, and when a greyling or a small trout comes into that lie, they will drive it out. My belief is that a salmon takes a bait because it is annoyed with it. If you spend enough time annoying them, you can make them take it.'

Having explained that salmon lie in deep pools, facing the current, Dick went on. 'You have to know your river,' he said. 'If you know where to look and what to look for, you can see them. With a salmon you look for a head or a tail or a dorsal fin, with trout you look for the whole fish because that is what you are going to see. Mind you, some people can see fish and some can't.'

Dick has constructed wooden groynes in the river to act as artificial salmon lies, lines of closely-placed poles at an angle to the bank, stretching out for a few feet into the water.

'I want to keep the salmon here, you see,' he said. 'If you give them somewhere to lie, then your rods have every opportunity to catch them. Every keeper wants to hold the salmon in his stretch for as long as possible.

'Salmon are lazy fish,' he went on. 'They don't like to work hard to stay in their lie, whereas trout will work very hard to stay where there is food. I don't enjoy salmon fishing so much myself: it seems to me that every man has a hunting instinct and if you see a trout feeding, that fish becomes a target. If you can present a fly correctly to that fish, it will take it: that is what gives me the satisfaction. With salmon fishing, although you might know where a salmon is lying up, you are fishing blind.'

We walked across a bridge and stopped to look down into the river. Long green strands of carrot weed streamed out under the clear water and one loose clump of weed moved steadily downstream. The river is deceptive: it looks quite still, but in fact it is running at about three or four miles an hour.

We came round a corner and found two more fishermen with long faces. They were sitting on a bench consoling themselves with cans of white wine, but they jumped to their feet like naughty schoolboys when they saw Dick coming. He suggested they tried a different pool and maybe a bit of fly-fishing. Which fly did he recommend?

'Thunder and Lightning,' he said, 'or Blue Charm? Hairy Mary? Stoat's Tail?'

The men listened and nodded gravely. They looked as if they wished Dick would go with them and catch a fish for them, but they could not quite get up the nerve to ask him. Dick wished them luck and went on his way.

A heron flew overhead and a sedge-warbler sang among the reeds. There were flowers everywhere, pink, white and purple comfrey, yellow pineapple mayweed, silver weed, creeping cinquefoil, St John's wort, crosswort, meadow rue, yellow rattle, valerian, water forget-me-not, and most delightful of all, lady's bedstraw, a tiny yellow flower with an enchanting smell. According to legend it was on a bed of these flowers that Mary lay in the stable at Bethlehem. There were spotted and early purple orchids in the water-meadows, marsh woundwort, purple loosestrife and meadowsweet – miles of meadowsweet all along the banks.

Dick Houghton tried to record every flower as it appeared one year, but had to give up because there were so many he could not keep up.

'I plant quite a few wild flowers myself every year,' he said. 'I've a few patches of cowslips, although of course they're over now. In one patch there were just two flowers when I arrived here sixteen years ago. Now there are twenty-seven. That's not bad, is it?'

There was a scarlet tiger moth on the comfrey flowers.

'Their caterpillars feed on the comfrey plants at the time of the cuckoos,' Dick said, 'and those caterpillars are the cuckoo's main diet – certainly round here. Everything has its life-cycle, you see. That is one thing that fascinates me about nature – the way she provides.'

As we walked back towards Dick's cottage, a fisherman suddenly appeared round the corner, heading in the same direction. His face said it all. He had caught a fish and was hurrying back to weigh his catch and record it in the record book. Every fish caught is entered with the weight, the bait used, the place caught and the name of the man who caught it. If any fisherman is not sure exactly where he made his catch, there is a map on the wall with all the pools clearly marked – Ward's Pool, Lone Tree, Swan's Nest, Forty Twenty, Joan's Pool. The fish was a salmon, caught with a prawn and it weighed 7 pounds. It was a grilse (first time back from the sea) Dick said, and a female. You could tell it was a female, he explained, because their faces are more rounded than the cock fishes. You could also tell that it was 'fresh' – not long come from the sea.

'When a salmon first comes in, it is a beautiful bluey-silver,' he said, 'but as it swims upstream it becomes a bit duller and the anal fin turns from being completely translucent to showing dark lines along the bones.'

The fisherman who had caught it was so excited that he could hardly decide whether to weigh it, hose it down, or write in the book first.

'It's nice, isn't it?' he said over and over again. 'Isn't it a nice one?'

The largest fish ever landed on the Itchen was a $43\frac{1}{4}$-pound salmon caught in a snowstorm in April, 1958. It rose to a fly, which it did not take, and was caught with a plug. The river was in flood and the salmon made one tremendous run and then swam on to the bank where it was caught.

Towards evening the trout were rising well. Dick explained that to catch one you would need to know what they were feeding on, which would depend on the time of day, the weather conditions and the time of year. For instance, on that particular evening they were feeding on sedge flies, but later on you would have to watch for the sherry spinners to start to move upstream, flying high towards white water to lay their eggs. Once they have laid their eggs, they die and come floating back downstream, dead. You can see them flying up and you can see them floating down; when you see that, you change your fly to a sherry spinner.

'As the sherry spinners start floating down,' Dick said, 'the blue-winged olive flies are starting to hatch and the fish will start feeding on the hatching nymphs as they reach the surface, so as well as a Dun you have to have a hackled blue fly which is usually fished within the surface film. Trout rise differently for different flies. It's a different sound, a different rise form and so on. I *know* when a trout changes what it's feeding on.'

.The difference between a true dry fly and one fished within the surface film is that a dry fly is tied with cock hackle – the feathers from the neck of a cock bird – and the fly you fish in the surface film is tied with hen's hackle, because it is softer. You have to have the right materials.

'In May and June iron-blue flies are used here,' Dick said, 'which are tied with mole fur, because that is the way the old boys used to do it back in the 1860s and that is the right way to do it.

'Another fly used in this area is the Tups Indispensable, which is tied with fur from a tup – the pinkish fur from the scrotum of a tup lamb – and you can fish that dry or in the surface film.

'In my opinion the size is very important with artificial flies. I don't think the fish see things magnified through the water, but I think that when a natural fly, which would weigh about one gram, lands on the water, it makes a slight indentation on the surface film and your artificial fly has to have exactly the same effect.

'I've a friend who is a very keen fisherman,' Dick told me. 'He once filled a bath full of water, lay down in it and got someone to place different artificial flies on the surface so that he could see what indentation they made. He was getting the trout's eye view, you see!' Mr Houghton clapped his hands together and laughed with delight.

What did he find out?

'He wouldn't tell me,' Dick said, still laughing.

Every month during the fishing season, Dick Houghton stocks up the river with fifty trout of catchable-size and every October he puts in seven thousand salmon parr of between four and seven inches in length. These will change to smolts and run to the sea between April and June the following year.

'The official estimate is that between 2 and 15 per cent of those fish will get back to the river safely to spawn,' Dick said. 'The experts say that the smells of the river become implanted in the smolts as they make their way down to the sea. So when they come back the next year, or the year after that, all they have to remember is to turn right at Southampton. If they turn left, they end up in the river Test, and that would be too bad, wouldn't it?' said Dick Houghton, smiling broadly.

AUGUST

By August the familiar footpaths have almost disappeared under a fresh crop of mettlesome nettles and a tangle of thistles, burs and teasels, all trying their best to attach themselves to anything that moves. Reproduction is running riot. The air is full of seeds silently colonising new territory with every breeze. The birds are mostly silent, except for the house-martins, perched in lines on the telephone wires, chattering earnestly. Surely they cannot be planning their journey south already? Yes, they can. That impersonation of musical notes into which they have arranged themselves is probably the first few bars of Wotan's farewell to Brünnhilde. Sight-reading house-martins is a frustrating business: no sooner have you got the first chord sorted out than they all change places.

An endless roar from the corn fields means that harvesting has begun and the combines are out. Combine harvesters are the duchesses of farming machinery. Formidable ladies who, in spite of their size, cannot be persuaded to come out until the dew is off the grass, and sometimes refuse to move at all, even though the farmers have spent many hours through the winter months checking that their internal workings are in good order. And when the great day comes and the sun is shining and the corn is ripe and their proud owners switch on, the suspense is terrible. Will she go? If, since they last looked, a family of mice have made their home under her skirts and chewed up the insulation on the electric components, the answer is no.

Once coaxed into action, the combines move across the fields in a cloud of dust, chopping off the ears of wheat, barley or rye and spewing out the stalks to be baled up later. Tractors bustle to and fro drawing high-sided trailers behind them into which the combines disgorge the precious, golden grain. Following the line of standing corn, the combines sweep across the fields, backing, bowing and advancing again at the corners with perfect dignity and a deafening roar. As one farmer put it, 'there's no conversation on a combine'. Farm labourers, dwarfed by the machines, jump up and down and shout instructions through the windows of the cab, where the driver sits, invisible, so that the great machines seem to move by themselves, gradually reducing the corn to a smaller and smaller square, and leaving the local rabbits in a state of shock. Startled ears stick up above the stubble all around – 'What's up, Doc?'

At this time of year the fate of the cereal farmers is in the hands of the gods.

'I'm never happy until the last combine pulls out of the last field,' Charles Amos said. 'You can't be sure of your harvest, until the grain is actually in store, but when that time comes, it is a wonderful feeling. That is when you get a real sense of achievement – seeing it there, in bulk . . . and it's even better if it pours with rain the next day,' he said, laughing.

As Alan Riddlestone drives back with the last load of wheat on his farm in Essex, he stops long enough to pick a leaf from a tree that has stood at the entrance to his farmyard for a hundred years. It is a ritual that was practised by his father and grandfather before him. 'All is safely gathered in. . . .'

In Dorset there are more dairy farms than anything else. Mike Chandler explained to me that most farmers had a stock unit and that most of those stock units were dairy. The reason is that grass grows more easily in the west of England because it has a higher rainfall than the east. Mike Chandler farms 900 acres near Moreton in Dorset.

'This is Thomas Hardy country,' he said. 'This is what he called The Vale of the Big Dairies where Tess came as a dairymaid in *Tess of the D'Urbervilles.*'

Mike Chandler has a dairy herd of 280 cows for which he allows 700 acres of land for grazing, silage and hay while he grows cereals on the remaining 200 acres, although the soil is light, which is, according to Mike, 'not the best land for growing cereals'. We were standing in one of his fields and Mike Chandler was explaining why you sometimes get patches of flattened corn scattered around a field. It looks for all the world as if a large animal has rolled there in the night and then disappeared without trace, but the explanation is that there might have been an accidental overlap of fertilisers there making the ground richer, or that the ground is wetter at that spot so that the corn springs up and the wind knocks it down. Every field has its peculiarities and it is up to the farmer to know his land. A farmer walking his land or standing, leaning over a gate and looking at it, is not lost in some quaint rural abstraction, but is learning as much from what he sees as an accountant would learn from reading a balance-sheet.

Mike Chandler's grown-up sons now do most of the running of the farm so he spends a lot of time advising other farmers about how to improve the quality not only of the countryside but also of their lives within in. He believes that conservation and commercial farming can, and will, live together.

'The landscape around us is not a "natural" countryside,' he said. 'It has been created by farmers. Whether we own our land or are tenant farmers, we are only here for a short time really and we must use our land in the best way we can. That's good stewardship, isn't it? Stewardship is the word I like to use. The look of the country matters to me and to a lot of my colleagues. The look can either be 'suburban tidiness', which I do my best to avoid, or it can be more of a variety without causing problems agriculturally. There needs to be variety — that is what people come to the countryside for. When I grew up, we farmers were appreciated simply because we were producing the nation's food and were doing so under difficult conditions. Now we are looked upon as producers of rather expensive surpluses. We've been getting a bad press. In the past I suppose farmers were motivated by the commercial aspects, but more and more of them are now taking an interest in conservation and that is good — it is good public relations for the farming industry as a whole.'

Mike Chandler has seen a great many changes to farming in his lifetime.

'When did you last see a ploughed field?' he asked me. I had to think hard and that proved his point. 'In the old days the fields would be ploughed in December or January and they would stay like that until spring when the crops were sown. Now 90 per cent of cereals are sown in autumn. Immediately after the harvest, the land is ploughed and a couple of days later the seeds go in.'

The change to autumn sowing means that there are more green fields to be seen through the year, from the mustard and cress effect of the winter wheat and barley as it starts coming up in October, to the overall grass-like covering of the fields through the winter and early spring. But for those of us with a taste for the more austere beauty of a perfectly ploughed field, it is a loss.

'It seems to me,' Mike Chandler said, 'that farmers have become more and more dependent on machinery; they have been encouraged to invest in more machinery and the machines have got bigger and more complicated and to a certain extent we have replaced human ingenuity with brute force and ignorance. I don't suppose the younger generation would agree with that, but that is my opinion.'

When the heather comes into bloom there will be bees busy collecting the heather honey: not necessarily local bees . . . quite likely not local bees. The bee farmers take their hives hundreds of miles for the heather harvest at the end of the summer.

'What we have in this country is a lot of migratory bees following the crops,' Bill Flynn, the bee-master, said.

The heather harvest is a bonus for those who live within striking distance of the moors or the mountains. The main flow of honey for the bee-keepers will have come in June and July, something like thirty pounds of honey from each hive, although in fact the bees will have produced four times that much as they eat three-quarters of the honey they produce to keep themselves alive.

Leo Hiam takes his hives to the Welsh Mountains for the heather. If it is flowering well, he will take as many as 500 hives, from which he will expect to collect four and a half tons of honey at the end of the season.

'If it's a good year, people seem to imagine that you'll have the hives full of honey,' Leo said. 'They seem to think the bees carry it back in two-gallon buckets.'

In fact it takes about 20,000 bee flights to collect one pound of honey. The bees fly within a radius of one and a half miles from the hive on each flight, which is almost the same, as Leo explained, as saying that 'a bee would have to fly to the moon and back for that pound of honey'. But of course a bee does not live long enough in summer to cover that staggering distance.

'They wear themselves out,' Leo said. 'They never rest and they never sleep. In summer a bee will only live for about six weeks.'

When Leo Hiam's bees arrive in Wales, they are not in the best of tempers after the long journey.

'When I open the hives, they come tearing out,' he said, 'and believe me they would sting anything that moved.' A Customs and Excise Officer discovered that for himself when he appeared out of nowhere just as Leo was releasing his bees.

'I warned him not to come near,' Leo said, 'but he wouldn't listen. He said he wanted to test the diesel in the truck and that I couldn't stop him.' Leo Hiam shook his head sadly at the folly of officials. 'He didn't seem to understand that it wasn't me that was going to stop him.'

What happened? 'The bees came out and I've never seen anyone disappear over a wall so fast in my life,' said Leo, with a small, satisfied smile.

The honey is produced in the hive from nectar brought in by the field bees. Nectar becomes honey when the moisture is taken out of it.

'You will hear this roaring noise. It's all the bees in the hive flapping their wings to dry out the nectar,' Leo said. 'Actually they flap their wings one way to make the honey and they flap their wings another way to ventilate the hive and keep the air circulating.'

This practice is called 'fanning' in polite bee circles. Outside the hive more bees are fanning, sending out scent beams from a gland in their bodies to guide the field bees home. Bill Flynn explained that it acts as a sort of scent radar which ensures that even when the hives are grouped close together, each bee gets back to its own hive.

In late August the bees begin to tidy up for the winter. The first thing they do is to get rid of the drones whose usefulness is at an end. The drones are starved of honey and when they are too weak to resist, they are tipped out.

'It sounds cruel, doesn't it?' said Bill apologetically.

Later on, at the end of the heather season, Leo Hiam goes and collects his bees to take them home for the winter. He lost a hive once on his way back from Wales.

'We had just passed Hereford when I happened to look in the rear-view mirror,' he said, 'and I noticed that one of the hives had fallen off the truck. I never thought I'd find it because it was pitch dark, but I turned round and a few miles back I saw a policeman standing in the road. Somebody had seen the hive fall and reported it, so this policeman had been called out of bed. He was wearing bedroom slippers and pyjamas under his uniform and he'd been stung on the ankle. He was a bundle of joy, I must say.'

Back home, the bee-keepers 'take off' the honey and feed the bees with thirty-five pounds of sugar per hive to keep them going through the winter.

'Bees are not like cows or sheep,' Leo said. 'When you go out to feed them, they are never pleased to see you. It's always the same old welcome.' His round, cheerful face looked almost sad for a moment. 'Not many people seem to like bees,' he said. 'I don't know why.'

In August the lambs born in the spring begin to go to market. In Welshpool sheep market, which is one of the largest in the United Kingdom, Tom Jones had been selling 50 of his lambs. He would be bringing 50 lambs to the market every week until the majority were sold and then the last few would be kept until the new year. We walked round to look at his lambs in their pens: they had already been auctioned and Mr Jones had the cheque in his pocket. This would be the last he would see of them, fine-looking animals, all of a similar size and alike as peas in a pod. I asked him how he felt about letting them go.

'This is business,' he said. 'That's the reason they were born after all.' Tom Jones is thirty-six years old, brisk and efficient, dark-haired and confident. 'With sheep, it's the moment of birth when business and nursing come closest,' he goes on. 'When it comes to selling them, I try not to look at them individually. I try not to look at their faces. Every now and then, of course, there will be a pet lamb, or one that has had something wrong with it which we've had to work hard on, and then it is different. Then they are friends as well as animals.'

We walked away from the market to where he had left the Land Rover and trailer that had brought the lambs from the farm. Only the sheepdog was left in the trailer now.

'He's called Nip,' Tom Jones said, pulling a disapproving face. 'That was my father's choice. He'd had a good dog of that name at one time. My last dog was called Mot – that's Tom backwards, you see.'

Always short names?

'Oh yes,' said Tom. 'You can't start swearing in sentences can you?'

We drove through the gently undulating countryside of what used to be Montgomeryshire in mid Wales. The hills were rounded, green and sudden. On the way to his farm Tom Jones, whose first language is Welsh but who is equally articulate in English, explained that his grandfather had originally bought the farm in a valley which was described at the time as 'this wild and desolate place' (*cwm gwyllt, anghysbell* in Welsh). Since then the farm has gradually been expanded and improved until today it is able to graze 1,800 breeding ewes and 120 suckler cows.

131

Tom Jones and his brother, who now run the farm together, are still making improvements. In one year they planted 5,000 softwood and 1,000 hardwood trees and they have also installed drainage on one 50-acre field at a cost of £30,000 which was a big investment, even with government grants.

'I am locked into this land because of tradition and responsibilities,' Tom Jones said. 'My father and my grandfather farmed here and although I know I could get a good price for the farm, I could never sell, especially now that I have a son of my own to follow me.'

Unless you have been brought up in a Welsh-speaking community, the Welsh language appears impenetrable when it is written down, but it is music when it is spoken. We drove through 'Cwn Nant Yr Eira', which means 'The Valley of the Snow Stream'. In this valley Tom Jones's father had sold 1,000 acres to a commercial forestry concern and the result was a mass of conifer trees, closely packed together in straight lines, which, as Tom said, 'is monotony in any language'. But the road constructed by the forestry people had at least made it easier for the Jones family to get from one part of their farm to the other. We drove through the forest and to the top of a hill, where we stopped by a ruined stone cottage, *Pen-ffridd* (Top of the High Ground). Tom told me that only a generation ago a couple had lived in this cottage and brought up fourteen children. Pacing round the picturesque ruin and translating as he went along, Tom Jones, who is also a writer, quoted part of a poem he had written about it in Welsh.

' ". . . a wall, that was a room, that was a building, that was a house, that was a home. Inside a pregnant sheep is lying where a mother once raised her family, and cattle are grazing on the carpet of weeds in the parlour. . . ."

'Conservation is not just to do with plants and hedges,' he continued. 'It is to do with people too.'

Tom Jones is not only a farmer and writer but also a spokesman for various conservation bodies and the local farmers. As such, he would like to see more help given to the small hill farmers whose communities are threatened.

'If the hill farmers are forced out of business, then the schools and the chapels and the shops would disappear too, and with them would go the language and that would be a disaster, although I know some people wouldn't agree with me.' Tom believes a way must be found to encourage these people to give the public more access to their land. 'This is a social policy, really, not a farming policy,' he explained. 'This is the most beautiful landscape we can offer. People like to walk in the wilderness of the tops, to see the stone walls and the hedges and the sheep grazing on the upper slopes. That is where the beauty is.

'But I would like to see the hill farmers actually encouraged, financially, to farm in the way they have always done and to preserve the countryside and their traditional way of life.'

We drove back to the farm to have a look at the cattle. Tom Jones and his brother calve their suckler cows in both spring and autumn and the autumn calving had just begun.

'The fields round the farm are little hospital wards really,' Tom said. 'Then, when the calves are a few days old, they are moved with their mothers into another field where we can keep our eye on them, and then, gradually, they move further and further away until eventually the cow meets up with the bull again and comes back to the farm for the next calving. In the old Welsh tradition they are moved from the high ground to the low ground and back again to get the best of the grass all through the year – their lives are a circle, *Hafod* and *Hendre*, summer and winter, year in, year out.

We walked through the field next to the farm where the cows about to calve or those which had just calved were grazing.

'I had an ideal afternoon yesterday,' Tom said. 'One of my young cows produced a male Charolais calf and a Welsh black heifer brought me a black heifer calf. That's the future, you see. I had a lovely afternoon.

'She cost me £600 last year with a calf at foot,' Tom said, talking about one cow in the field with a calf – a black and white Hereford-cross-Friesian. 'Now she's produced another calf, so, by next year, all being well, if she produces a third calf, I will start to get something back for my money. There's not many people would put up £600 and wait three years before they saw anything for it, is there? Only farmers.

'She's got a calf in the grass somewhere,' Tom said, pointing out a blue-roan cow standing looking at us with her back to some rushes. 'But she's not going to tell us where it is.' We went looking and found the calf curled up in the rushes, just a few hours old. 'It's a heifer,' Tom said smiling with pleasure. 'I decided to try out a Belgian Blue bull on her as an experiment. Now in three years' time I can put this calf to a Belgian Blue and then I'll have a three-quarter Belgian Blue. . . . If this little calf had been a bull, that would have been the end of the exercise.' He looked at the cow. 'The calf's been suckling too, that's good. You can tell because the cow's two back teats are smaller, do you see?'

We walked past a black Welsh cow that had not yet calved.

'She's only got one quarter (one teat) working and this will be her last calving,' Tom said. 'I've kept her on for sentiment, if you like. I hope she has a heifer calf so I'll have something to remember her by.'

Behind the fence on higher ground were the cows who had calved in the past week; one of them was bellowing continuously.

'There must be something wrong,' Tom said, 'We'd better take a look.'

As we walked through the gate the cows were moving slowly up the field on the opposite side. One small calf trotted beside his mother with a graceful, fluid movement, more like a colt than a calf, while the others see-sawed along stiff-legged, in that characteristic rocking gait.

The bellowing cow was out of sight, but making so much noise that it was not difficult to find her. She was standing by a fence on the far side of the field where her calf was lying on the ground. The calf was a reddish colour (fathered by a Charolais bull and out of a Hereford-cross-Friesian mother) and was scouring (suffering from diarrhoea). It was too weak to stand and lying there helplessly, with its huge dark eyes and long ears, it looked more like a fawn than a calf.

'It's a mystery why it should have had such a severe attack,' Tom said, bending down and kneeling by its side.

'It was born out-of-doors where there is less risk of infection and it certainy suckled after it was born, so it should have been protected by the colostrum in its mother's milk for at least ten days.' The mother moved in closer, watching Tom as he handled the calf; she was quiet now, head down, watching everything that happened.

'I'll have to go back to the farm and get something for it,' Tom said.

When he had gone the mother cow moved back to the top of the hill, looking after him, bellowing again, neck stretched out, mouth wide open. By the fence it was very quiet. The only sound came from a stream somewhere deep between the trees on the other side of the fence . . . a faint sound of water trickling away, like hope.

Tom came back with a syringe of antibiotics and a bottle of something to replace some of the fluid lost by the calf.

'It will be suffering from dehydration, you see,' Tom explained. He picked up the calf's head. 'Her nose is very cold,' he said, 'and her mouth is tight like dead people's mouths go.'

The calf tried to struggle away from him, getting to its feet and staggering a few steps before he caught it again. When he had poured all the fluid down the calf's throat, Tom gave it the injection of antibiotics and stood back.

'It's eyes are quite bright, aren't they?' he said, 'and it's holding its head up. It doesn't look too bad. We'll come back later.'

An hour later we went back. The calf's head was flat on the ground and its legs were sprawled out untidily over the grass. It was worse, weaker, colder. Tom had brought more fluid, a glucose mixture this time, and he lifted the calf's head and poured some into her mouth. Every time he let go, the calf's head fell back onto the ground.

'You've got to be careful to get it down their throats and not into the lungs,' he said. 'I should have brought a teat with me so it doesn't lose the instinct to suck.' When the bottle was empty he knelt down and gently stroked the calf.

The sun was going down and by the fence it was suddenly very much colder.

'We'd better take her in,' Tom said.
We picked her up between us and carried her to the pick-up truck where we laid her in the back. She didn't move. The mother cow was weaving backwards and forwards around us and around the truck. Tom said that if she saw where the calf was, she would

135

follow us. We got into the truck and Tom drove very slowly across the field. The cow did follow, trotting, and then, when she realised we were going to leave the field, she overtook us and tried to charge the front of the moving truck to stop it, although once we were on the track leading down to the farm, she followed us again. Tom drove straight into the yard where there was a row of outbuildings. We carried the calf into a cubicle in one of the buildings and covered the small shape with straw. It lay curled up tight and very still. Outside the cow was bellowing again, not knowing where we had gone, and was running up and down the yard, frantic with anxiety. It took two of us to guide her towards the right door.

'*Stop her. Assert yourself,*' Tom called urgently as she nearly barged past me at the last minute.

Once the mother cow was safely in the stall, Tom went to get the infra-red lamp they use at lambing time and connected it up so that the heat was directed onto the calf. We stood in the next stall looking down over the wooden barrier at the small form, now lit by a dull, red glow. We watched for a long time, but the calf did not move and all the time the mother cow was standing with her head lowered, making small, poignant noises in her throat.

'We can't give her another injection until ten o'clock tonight,' Tom said, nodding at the calf. 'The antibiotics have to work their way through her system before they will start to do anything. It's hard to wait, but that's all we can do.'

I had been told by another farmer that a sick calf really tears your insides out.

'First of all it's a blow to your pride,' he had said, 'then it's a terrible blow to your feelings, and last, and I do mean last, it's expensive.' I had thought he had sounded as if he was talking sense, but now that I was involved, even at second hand, I could see how right he had been. Alan Riddlestone's words echoed in my head: 'When a calf needs an injection, it needs it yesterday'. How long had that mother cow been calling for help while Tom was driving back from market and his brother was working on another part of the farm? Had we been in time?

'I don't know what else I can do for her at the moment,' said Tom. 'Remember I was talking about what a lovely day I'd had yesterday? That'll teach me to boast, won't it?'

In his book, *Moor town*, Ted Hughes includes a poem called 'Little Red Twin':

> *We pump more glucose water down her daughter's*
> *helpless glug-glug. Sundown polishes the hay*
> *Propped on her crumpled leg, her sunk fire*
> *Only just in. Now some sacks across her,*
> *To keep in the power of the glucose*
> *Through night's barespace leakage. The minutes*
> *Will come one by one, with little draughts,*
> *And feel at her, and feel her ears for warmth.*
> *And reckon up her chances, all night*
> *Without any comfort. We leave her*
> *To her ancestors, who should have prepared her*
> *For worse than this. The smell of the mown hay*
> *Mixed with moonlight with driftings of honeysuckle*
> *and dog-roses and foxgloves, and all*
> *The warmed spices of the earth*
> *In the safe casket of stars and velvet*
> *Did bring her to morning. And now she will live.*

Next morning Tom Jones rang me up to say that the calf was on its feet again. . . . I was glad.

SEPTEMBER

The leaves change colour little by little. Walking along a tree-lined country lane, you notice that just a few branches here and there have turned to gold or red or brown. They are like the banners of a mediaeval army, richly coloured antique standards, glowing bravely in the golden mellow sun. Across the fields the woods still look green, but the mists that cling close to the earth give those same woods an illusion of remoteness. It is as if summer is withdrawing, retreating step by step while you watch. And then one morning there is a touch of cold steel in the air, a delicate warning from old winter's men-at-arms that it will not always be like this. Hang out more banners. The dark days are coming.

> '. . . I will reach
> For rich autumn's robe, red
> My pride and grieving . . .'
>
> (Elizabeth Daryush)

The look of the fields is changing day by day as more crops are harvested and the land is ploughed and re-seeded in one long extended effort that often goes on far into the evening. The arable farmers told me that nowadays 'it's all rush.' With the change to autumn planting, 'it's a case of racing to get the seeds in as quickly as possible'. But, even in all the rush, farmers can still take pride in their ploughing. The plough is one of the most evocative images of the countryside, and 'ploughing is perhaps the most basic of all the operations upon which systematic farming depends', as Roy Brigden, Keeper of the Museum of English Rural Life at the University of Reading, says, in the introduction to his book, *Ploughs and Ploughing*. The turning over of the top few inches of soil does two things – it speeds up the process of decay in the plant matter remaining in the soil after harvesting and it exposes the soil below, creating a seed-bed for the new crop. Roy Brigden goes on to say:

> *The ability to plough a field well has always been regarded as more of an art than a mere skill. As well as the technique and experience, the stamina and doggedness, and the mastery over beast or machine, there had to be an infusion of natural, indefinable ability. This was the quality that created local heroes at the popular ploughing matches of the nineteenth century, when neighbouring rivalries whipped-up much spirited competition. It was also the quality that raised the ploughman and his team above the common anonymity of rural society, confirming a degree of agricultural nobility upon both. A good ploughman was worth the extra wages he received. A badly ploughed field could not be hidden but remained on public view for all to see and scorn.*

An acre was a land measurement arrived at originally because that was the amount of land a man and his oxen could plough in one day; but with a tractor, a modern farmer could cover up to something like ten acres, according to Alan Riddlestone, 'if he hammered on a bit'. Tractors came into general use after the Second World War, but it was not until the early 1980s that they were built with cabs on them to keep out the wind and the rain.

'I've been out in the fields ploughing and the water would be almost running out of my pants,' an old farm labourer said . . . not that getting wet discouraged him at all. 'I love ploughing best of all the jobs around the farm,' he continued. 'I loved to watch the change in the soil and the way the weeds went under out of sight. Ploughing satisfies your mind.'

140

Earlier in his life the same man had been a waggoner's mate, walking behind a team of horses all day and when he got home at night and took his socks off, 'the skin used to come off with them'. It was the rough clods of earth underfoot that did it. The plough-man in Gray's *Elegy* who homeward plodded 'his weary way' probably had bad feet too.

Alan Riddlestone likes tractors. He likes them so much that, apart from the up-to-date ones he uses on the farm in Essex, he keeps a collection of older models in the barn and needs no encouragement whatsoever to start them up just for the pleasure of hearing them judder and roar. Deafening stuff. Alan was taught how to plough by his uncle.

'He liked to see a straight furrow,' Alan said. 'If you made a mistake you'd be the talk of the village and other villages round here for twenty miles.' His uncle took him out to a field at the back of the farm and taught him how to position himself absolutely square to start with, and then to begin with a good long straight stretch of the field.

'It's all a matter of judgement,' he said. 'You fix your eyes on some landmark directly opposite and make for that.' He leaned forward. 'You've heard the story about the old ploughman have you? He took up his position, looked across the field and saw a white marker in just the right place, so off he went. Halfway across he seemed to be well out of line and he couldn't understand it. Then he realised that his white marker was a seagull.' Alan leant back and laughed. 'But they're always awkward shapes, the fields. It's very seldom you get a square field. They must have all been on the bottle when they marked them out,' he said, still laughing.

A solitary tractor driver, ploughing a field with only a few seagulls for company, is a man lost to the world. Inside the cab of a modern tractor he is cut off not only by space, but by sound. Surrounded by a silent panorama of brown soil, distant trees and sky, the driver is cocooned within the noise of the engine, the radio (standard equipment in modern tractors) and even a CB radio on the most up-to-date farms. Alan Riddlestone prefers, however, to listen to the noise of the engine.

'I like to plough with the windows of the cab open so I can hear if a bearing is going,' he said. 'Though of course with the windows open you get all the noise from the seagulls. They are right up your backside, screeching all the time.'

The Electricity Board have put up pylons on part of Alan Riddlestone's land and they pay him £20 a year per pylon. But if he had the choice he would much rather do without the money and the pylons because they make ploughing difficult, along with the added nuisance of Electricity Board officials trampling over the crops to service them.

'There was an electrician working on a pylon one day when I was ploughing,' said Alan, 'and after a while he shouted down, "You've been doing nothing but go up and down, up and down, up and down. It must drive you mad." I told him I'd rather be ploughing than perched up on a pylon any day. . . .'

Each field should be ploughed one way one year and the opposite way the next, otherwise the earth would be turned over in the same direction every time and the field would eventually have a deep trough on one side and a large mound of earth on the other.

'If you started on the right-hand side of the field one year, you are supposed to start on the left-hand side the next year,' Alan Riddlestone said. 'That is, if you can bloody well remember where you did start.'

The new, heavier farm machinery can now sow direct into the stubble after harvesting without the need to plough the land first. It would be a pity if the oldest of all farming skills were to disappear completely. A well-ploughed field not only 'satisfies the mind' of the man who does it, it satisfies the eye of the onlooker too.

What has happened to all those lovely old fruit orchards, those graceful apple and pear trees standing in their grassy fields with sheep grazing underneath them? The answer is the Dutchman. A man called Dan Neuteboom, who came to England in the 1970s and showed the British fruit growers how to grow top fruit. Instead of having between 75 and 200 trees to the acre, all about 40 feet high, Dan Neuteboom demonstrated that you could plant 900 trees to the acre, small ones, and get a lot more fruit.

Fruit farmers buy their trees from commercial nurseries at one year old when they are 'Maidens' – either 'Maiden Whips' (single stems) or 'Feathered Maidens' (trees with small branches which can be trained into shape more quickly).

'In the sixties the fruit farmers had it easy,' Graham Tapp, a fruit farmer, said to me. 'You could sell anything. It used to be thought that all you had to do was to plant your trees, leave them for six years and then go along and gather your crop. When Dan Neuteboom came along, he took us all to the cleaners.'

Graham Tapp is a serious-minded and caring young man, but a hard taskmaster as far as his trees are concerned.

'I plant all my trees by hand,' he said. 'If you don't plant a tree properly in the first place, you will always have a sick, backward tree. Eighteen years of problems – eighteen years because that is their life-span. We're pushing them hard and trees, like everything else, wear out.'

In September, when the fruit is hanging heavy from the trees, how does Graham Tapp know when his apples are ready for picking? Pop out and try one? Graham gave me a pitying look and explained.

'About three weeks before I would expect to start picking,' he said, 'I take an apple, hold it by its stalk and its "eye" and then cut it round its equator. Then I give it the starch/iodine test: I dip the fruit in the iodine and the starch in the fruit turns black. Every morning and every evening I do the same test on another apple and the black area increases. Then, one day, there is less black, which means that the starch is beginning to turn to sugar, and when the black area decreases to 80 per cent of the maximum recorded, the fruit is ready to pick.'

I was sorry I had asked.

Once the fruit is ready it should really, for perfection, be picked within hours but, as nobody can pick an orchard as quickly as that, a reasonable compromise is to get the fruit in within a day or two. The pickers are summoned to the orchards – housewives many of them, who bring a bit of light-hearted banter and a lot of laughter to the serious business of harvesting apples. The pickers are paid by the bulk bin, 48 inches long, 40 inches wide and 22 inches deep, which holds 640 pounds of apples or 700 pounds of pears. Transferring the fruit into the bins is a delicate operation because if it is allowed to fall in the fruit will bruise.

'People are getting more fussy about their fruit,' said Graham Tapp. 'They want perfectly shaped fruit with no blemishes whatsoever.'

A good fruit farmer knows exactly how each of his trees has cropped.

'I have 7,000 trees and I know each one personally,' Graham Tapp said. 'I can spot a sick tree long before the obvious signs of wilting leaves or shedding bark become apparent.'

Graham went on to explain that a tree which has cropped well will have produced very little growth, so when the time comes for pruning great care needs to be taken. 'Even ten years ago people did not understand that the more you cut a tree, the harder it will grow, and that means it will grow more wood instead of producing more fruit. Pruning fruit trees used to be a job left to any farm-workers short of something to do in the winter. Vast armies of ignorant people were let loose into the orchards to cut out bits of wood,' he said sorrowfully. 'All wrong. Pruning fruit trees is a job for experts.'

In September Venning Davey's cows start to calve on his farm in Blisland in Cornwall. Venning Davey has 250 acres of grass, 100 milking cows and 150 'followers' which are the by-products of the milking herd. Because he has sufficient grass, Venning rears all the calves that are born and keeps them either as replacements for the milking herd or to sell as beef at about two years old.

However, his main priority is milk. You have to produce calves to keep cows milking: after calving a cow's milk yield is at its peak for three months and then it begins gradually to decline until two months before the next calf is due when it dries up altogether. In a tiny, dark partition just off the milking parlour, Venning sits down every day to record the yield of every cow on the cows' record cards, and at the end of the week he draws a graph of the average milk yield of the herd.

Every cow should calve once every 365 days.

'She has to be a terrific good cow to warrant going over the twelve months with her,' Venning explained. 'She's eating her head off and producing nothing – no calf, no milk. And she's upsetting my seasonal pattern.'

The seasonal pattern of calving has changed from spring to autumn for dairy farmers like Venning, because the Milk Marketing Board introduced seasonality adjustments to their milk cheques which made it more profitable to produce the highest yields of milk during the winter months.

Fortunately cows are not seasonal breeders like sheep. When the calves arrive is nothing to do with the cows' habit, it is largely the farmers' choice. However, in one respect, autumn calving presents a real challenge to Venning Davey. He replaces twenty of the dairy herd every year with heifers he has bred himself and, because these heifers were born in autumn, they have to calve at two years old instead of two and a half.

'That,' says Venning, 'is another discipline altogether. That takes exceptionally good management.'

Venning Davey took over the farm in 1953. He started with twenty cows, six acres of potatoes, twenty sows and three hundred sheep. But then, as the pressure increased to produce more and more in order to stay solvent, he realised that he would have to specialise and concentrate on just one or two things. Venning chose milk with beef production as a by-product because he liked cows.

'And 'tis true that what you like you are best at,' he said.

Some of the cows he has now are direct descendants of his original herd and having reared every calf himself he knows every one of his cattle as an individual: 'They're not just numbers. Every one is different.' When one of his milking herd has to go to market at the end of its working life, he does not like it, but he says that when you are born in the country birth and death are both natural things. He is hurt by the fact that some people who do not understand farming think that cattle farmers who rear animals for slaughter have no compassion at all.

'These animal rights people think they are the only ones with feelings,' he said, 'but they're not.'

The way Venning Davey manages his herd has been thought out to the last detail. Since a cow's gestation period is nine months, most of the milking herd are artificially inseminated in January from a Friesian bull.

'In the end you don't find perfection anywhere, so I go for the best I can,' Venning said. 'But even if you put the two best beasts you can find together, you don't always get the result you hoped for.'

That is the chance that any breeder takes when he sets a lot of genes swilling around together and then stands back to see what happens. In order to obtain the heifers he requires, among his new-born calves, to act as replacements for the milking herd, Venning Davey puts sixty-five of his Friesian dairy cows in calf to a Friesian bull.

'Some years you get a run of heifers and sometimes you get a run of steers,' he said. 'But over about five years it seems to even itself out. Just like human babies; they even themselves out between boys and girls, give or take a few, don't they?' The heifers not needed for the dairy herd – and all the steers – will be bred for beef, so the bull who fathers them also has to have a record of producing good beef.

'I'm using Friesians as a dual-purpose animal here,' Venning said.

The rest of the milking herd are artificially inseminated from a Limousin bull because Venning believes that a Limousin-cross-Friesian produces the sort of beef the housewives are looking for. He adds, however, that every farmer has his own idea on the subject – 'We're very individualistic, we farmers.'

That, supposing that every service 'holds', takes care of the dairy herd, but then comes the tricky matter of the dairy herd replacements, still only fifteen months old, who have to be got into calf so that they, too, will start producing milk when their calves are born. For these heifers Venning brings in a North Devon bull in December and leaves him with the heifers for eight weeks.

'At the end of that time, the bull goes tripping up the ramp into the lorry and on to his next port of call as jolly as you like,' Venning said. 'What a life.'

The choice of a North Devon bull was taken after careful consideration. A Charolais, Hereford or Limousin would probably give Venning more profit on the beef from the calves and a Friesian would produce more Friesians, but Venning's first concern is the welfare of his heifers and he does not consider that any of these breeds would make for easy calving, considering the age of the heifers, whose first calf this will be.

Watching a calf coming into the world is always a thrilling sight, but Venning believes in leaving his cows to themselves as much as possible when they are calving.

'We look in every twenty minutes or so and if all is well we don't interfere,' he said, 'although obviously, over the year, we help a lot of calves into the world.'

Within half an hour of being born the calf should be on its feet and drinking the vital colostrum from its mother. Scientists who have analysed colostrum have found that it has all the same components as milk but in much higher quantities. In cases of emergency there are now substitutes on the market that can be fed to calves in place of the mother's colostrum, but Venning Davey believes that it is not only the content of the milk which is important; he believes that if the new-born calf can suck the milk from the cow it is better for it, because it comes out frothy and full of air-bubbles.

After only two days Venning separates the cows from their calves: he is sure that the longer you leave a cow and calf together, the more the cow will fret when you take it away.

'People say it is cruel,' he said, 'but I think it is much kinder to do it then. After a week,' Venning continued, 'wherever you hide that calf, the cow will keep going back to the place where she last saw it and roaring for it. She's upsetting herself and the rest of the herd.'

Venning rears all the calves himself, teaching them to drink by the old and well-tried method of getting them to suck his fingers and then gradually lowering his hand into a bucket of milk until the calf catches on and starts to drink.

'That's another reason for separating the cow and her calf after a couple of days,' Venning said. 'If you leave it any longer than that, you can have the most awful job getting the calf to drink from a

147

bucket. They've got it firmly in their heads that the only way to get food is to suck.'

New-born calves are as appealing, trusting and playful as any young animals. Venning had a young bullock once who became particularly attached to him and, as it turned out, did him a good turn. The herd had been grazing in a field in front of the farmhouse one afternoon when they took it into their heads to wade across a stream and climb up the opposite bank onto another farmer's land.

'Bullocks always want to be where they're not,' Venning said. 'Wherever you put them, they want to be somewhere else. If I ever leave a few of them in the barn, the ones outside like nothing better than to let them out. Bullocks are just as clever as horses at undoing bolts and catches and pieces of string you know.'

Venning heard about his straying bullocks and set off to bring them home. But when he had rounded them up and got them as far as the edge of the stream, they decided that they did not like the look of the steep bank and galloped off again. This happened three times and the situation was getting serious: it would have been a six-mile walk home by road and it was getting dark. Venning decided that animals that could not be driven might just possibly be led. He called his pet bullock to him, led it to the bank of the stream and then, without any hesitation, jumped in himself and started wading across. Halfway over he looked back to see the bullock standing on the bank with all the others clustered round him. He called him and while Venning watched, the bullock put his head up in the air and jumped into the water. Venning Davey's usually serious, lined face lit up with pleasure at the memory.

'I wouldn't have believed it if I hadn't been watching, but I swear he shut his eyes before he jumped,' he said. 'And of course as soon as he jumped all the others followed him.'

The first rush of milk after calving can give a cow milk fever. There is no warning, no way of preventing it and it is horribly dramatic. One minute the cow seems perfectly all right and the next she has gone down and looks as if she has gone for good. The treatment, however, is quick and equally dramatic.

'You inject magnesium straight into the vein, and if you went out to a cow lying in the field and gave it an injection, by the time you had walked back to the gate, the cow would probably be walking behind you, perfectly all right.'

Apart from the odd crashing cow, this is Venning Davey's favourite time of year. At last the results of all his careful planning are coming into being as the calves are born.

'This is when you get the real thrill of farming.' he said. 'And it's a marvellous feeling.'

Fifteen million visitors a year visit the Lake District, and in high season it is, according to one of the National Trust Wardens, 'heaving with people'. The National Trust owns one quarter of the Lake District National Park and their work involves keeping some of the most beautiful and popular areas open to everyone while at the same time preventing the destruction of the countryside through over-use. It is a delicate balance to maintain and, to the Trust's credit, they do their best to be as unobtrusive as possible. They construct paths and persuade people to keep to them by the careful siting of boulders or other natural-looking obstacles.

'We try to guide people without them being aware of it,' one of the National Trust's spokesmen in Ambleside said. 'We only feel we have succeeded in what we are trying to do when people are unaware that we have been there before them. It's the same with notices. If you see a notice you can be sure that we have tried to do without one and failed. I'm very much against negative notices, those starting with the word "Don't" or "No". I think it is much better, if you must have a notice, to start with the word "Please".'

As a charity the Trust's funds are limited, so they rely heavily on their members and on volunteers, who put in 6,000 working hours a year in the Lake District alone – building walls, laying paths and digging holes for some of the 3,000 broad-leaved trees planted by the Trust in the area every year.

By September, the crowds are thinning out and the fells are taking on the pink and tawny colours of autumn, soaring up behind the scattered buildings and at night, against a clear sky, forming a firm line of darkness round the villages. A stronghold.

It is easy to see why people are attracted to the Lake District; more difficult to imagine how it can be preserved unspoilt for the future. David Owen is a National Trust Warden with responsibility for 20,000 acres to the east of Windermere, including some of the 'honey pot' areas (as he described them). We went first to Stagshaw Gardens just outside Ambleside where he had been constructing a new path through the azaleas and rhododendron bushes for which the gardens are famous. The original path had been grass – 'too slippery', David Owen explained. They had tried wood-shavings first which looked good but got boggy, so then they had tried three different sorts of granite chippings before they were satisfied.

'I think we've got it right this time,' David Owen said, looking at the path critically, 'but it's still a bit loud at the moment. Shouts a bit, don't you think?'

Further up, away from the gardens the path winds its way through the trees towards the fell. This was originally a pack-horse trail and could have existed as far back as Roman times and, as David Owen said, 'they knew what they were doing'.

'Up here we've been careful to make the footpaths more rugged,' he said. 'People don't want a nice, twee path; if they're going up to the fell, they want a bit of rough. People think of the National Trust as being about big houses, Barbour jackets and green wellies, but in this area it's open spaces. That's what it's all about.'

He had found traces of culverts let into the ground to channel the water straight down the slope and had been rebuilding them to keep the water away from the path.

Jenkin's Crag is a well-known beauty spot halfway up the path through the trees. The crag is the perfect vantage point from which to look down over Lake Windermere and across the lake to the Langdale Pikes and Coniston Old Man in the distance. But so many people have followed the same route that the ground began to look like a grey desert and the trees were dying. So David Owen made a new path to the crag, a pitched path, which is like a dry stone wall on its side.

'Pitching is not like crazy paving,' Mr Owen explained. 'It's the same principle as an iceberg; only the tops of the stones show above the ground. This footpath will last forever. . . . It will see me out. Well out.' We looked at the view. 'Superb, isn't it?' David Owen said. 'Isn't that superb?'

It was.

'I heard recently about a revolutionary new invention in the United States,' he said, as we walked away. 'It's a new method of erosion control and they call it 'Rip Rap'. It's pitching that's what it is. It's been here since bloody Roman days.'

We drove to Cockshot Point just outside Bowness. Cockshot Point is a small park on the lakeside and, because it has a car- and coach-park at each end, it attracts the tourists who come to Bowness to drink as much as they can and then 'crash out' in the park. In summer they leave behind them nine sacks of litter every day.

'In the season we get hundreds and hundreds of tons of litter,' David said. 'I saw two youths throwing away a beer can one day. "What did you do that for?" I asked. "To give bastards like you something to do," they told me. What can you say?'

Driving up the Troutbeck Valley we passed several National Trust tenanted farms. According to David, the Trust's policy is to keep the same family in these farms through the generations wherever possible, but if the original family comes to a standstill, to install a new young family with children to start all over again.

The land on both sides of the road was rich pasture land.

'It's quality farming round here,' David Owen said, 'and most of the farmers care about their land, you know. They really do.'

The National Trust limewash the walls of their properties in the Lake District. This can be a long job, taking all the cement and modern paint off the walls.

'I can see some of the farmers wondering if it isn't all a waste of effort sometimes,' said David, 'but aesthetically the limewash is dead right and in the long run it's more practical, because it's porous and allows the damp to evaporate instead of becoming trapped inside the walls.'

The National Trust make their own limewash and lime plaster, described drily as 'very high technology' by one National Trust spokesman, showing me a picture of the workings – two old baths to mix it in and two pits underneath, one to hold the plaster and one to hold the wash.

The buildings are actually owned by the Trust, but their tenant farmers and Trust workers live in them, causing some confusion in the minds of sightseers.

'I know of one farmer,' David told me, 'who'd been out all day and his wife was upstairs with a migraine headache. When he got home he found a man in his kitchen making himself a cup of tea. The farmer wasn't very happy. "This is National Trust property isn't it?" the man asked, and the farmer said that it was. "Well, that's all right then," the man said, "I'm a member of the National Trust."

'The same thing happened to me,' David went on. 'We were just moving into our new cottage two years ago when a man and his family drove up and walked into the house. Nice man he was. I said to him "Can I help you?" and he said, "No, that's all right. We've just come to have a look round." '

David Owen had saved his most exciting piece of work until last. Up on Wansfell he and his team had made a discovery. When the fells had been divided up at the time of the enclosures in the late-eighteenth or early-nineteenth centuries, one of the farmers had evidently found himself with no way to move his sheep without crossing other farmers' fields, and so he had devised an 'underpass' for the animals. He built a sheep creep – an astonishing feat of construction – about four feet square, with dry stone walls and big slabs of slate for the roof which tunnelled under the fell for something like twenty-five feet. It is the only sheep creep of its kind that is known for certain to exist. David Owen and his team had cleared out the fallen stones from the entrance and found the tunnel still intact.

'Oh no, sheep wouldn't mind going through there,' David Owen said, as we peered into the opening, 'not as long as they could see daylight at the other end.'

Near the sheep creep he showed me an outbarn or fodder barn where the shepherd would have stayed with his flock during lambing time. The barn is next on David's list for rebuilding.

'There would have been a stone floor, and then a wooden floor overhead where they kept the hay,' he said. 'You can still see the opening where they'd have thrown the hay up into the loft.' We walked over to the half-ruined stone building. 'Can't you just imagine it?' David said enthusiastically. 'The shepherd up in that loft with just an oil lamp or something when it got dark. Just think how warm it must have been with all the hay and straw and all the sheep crowded in underneath. It must have been magic, mustn't it?'

I looked at the building standing ruggedly among all that spectacular scenery and listened to the wind singing over the 'forever' stones and agreed with him.

'You know what I'd like to do?' David Owen said. 'When this barn is rebuilt, I'd like to get some hay up here and bring in some lambs and sheep, and then get the local schoolchildren to come and see for themselves what it was really like. Wouldn't that be superb?'

OCTOBER

I saw old Autumn in the misty morn
Stand shadowless like Silence, listening
To Silence.

(Thomas Hood, *Ode: Autumn*)

The sight of bonfires and the smell of smoke set the seal on this time of year with the mists curling round the edges of the fields and the leaves on the trees burning scarlet, saffron, ochre and russet. Autumn has been called 'the Sabbath of the year'. There is a quietness over the fields now that the harvesting is over. As the day ends the sun sets in a spectacular red glow while the moon already rides high, a pale china-doll face staring down expressionlessly as wave after wave of rooks fly high overhead on their way home, cawing continuously, while from the woods the harsh, rusty voices of the pheasants sound over the darkening fields.

In autumn the woods are fat with pheasants. During the day they step delicately over the ploughed fields and tiptoe under cover when they sense a stranger's approach.

'You can always tell a hand-reared pheasant,' the keeper said. 'They walk like little old men. Wild pheasants stick their tails up and stride out.'

Twice a day the keeper comes to the woods and whistles up the pheasants to feed them: they know him and come to his call.

'They would not come to anyone else,' said Bob Carter, 'especially after the shooting season starts because then they get worldly-wise.'

The feeding places are always the same because the keeper likes to know where his birds are and to keep them as close as possible to the feeding grounds. The keepers scatter the food round and cover it with straw to make it more difficult for the birds to find – a game of hide-and-seek to keep them busy.

'The secret of rearing pheasants is to keep them occupied,' the keeper said, 'give them something to do. A bored pheasant is a restless pheasant.'

On the brown earth of the fields, the birds appear and disappear noiselessly; but inside the woods there is already a light carpet of dead leaves on the ground and every movement can be heard – 'Fields have eyes and woods have ears', it is said. The trees are changing every day, even hour by hour. The sun's rays strike lower, bringing a fresh brightness to the remaining leaves, an illusion of spring, and through the tall archways between the lines of trees, vividly contrasting colours of leaves blend and glow like stained glass.

> *Autumn, dark wanderer halted here once more,*
> *Grave roamer camped again in our light wood,*
> *With garments ragg'd, but rich and gorgeous-hued,*
> *With the same fraying splendours as before –*
> *Autumn, wan soothsayer, worn gypsy wise,*
> *With melancholy look, but bearing bold,*
> *With lean hard limbs careless of warmth or cold,*
> *With dusky face, and gloomed defiant eyes.*

(Elizabeth Daryush)

The fallow deer of the New Forest in Hampshire are at their most majestic in autumn when the bucks come into hard antler for the rutting season. Michael Clarke, Head Keeper in charge of deer control, explained that during the summer the male fallow deer keep themselves apart, but from the middle of September onwards, fallow deer of both sexes will be moving towards the traditional rutting stands for the October rut.

'Some of these rutting stands have been used for generations,' he said. 'I often wonder how the younger bucks know where they are. It's either instinct, or the fact that in the first year of their lives they would have visited the rutting stands with their mothers and the sight and sound is imprinted on their memories.'

The rutting stands are clearings among the trees where the master buck will take up his position in the centre. Around the perimeter the younger bucks will size one another up, challenge each other and fight, clashing antler to antler, head to head, pushing and wrestling to try to get the other off-balance. The master buck will not be challenged until the younger bucks sense that he is past his prime, but then, as Michael Clarke put it, you will get 'a real trial of strength under the chestnut trees'.

In *The Countryman's Guide to the South East* John Talbot White described a rut.

> *Watch a fallow buck standing in a clearing throwing his head rhythmically backwards and forwards uttering harsh warning groans from his swollen throat trying to dominate his territory with his show of aggression. Other bucks in the vicinity answer him until the whole arena echoes like a battlefield. Sixteen does are cropping quietly nearby until one suddenly breaks from the ring and bounds towards the woodland edge where another buck stands. The buck races after her, skidding in a sharp turn to head her off, butting her white inflated rump. She trots back, mewing plaintively. A young pricket approaches and the buck reacts violently. Another doe takes advantage of his distraction and escapes to another harem. The buck groans violently, beating his forelegs up and down in an exaggerated slow march like a soldier on parade.*

On Exmoor the red deer are a phenomenon. It is the only place in England where they flourish in the wild, and the reason for that, according to Maurice Scott, Joint Master of the Devon and Somerset Staghounds, is because they are hunted.

Maurice Scott, informally dressed on a non-hunting day, is a slightly melancholy-looking man who does not waste words, but speaks with authority on the subject of deer and the hunt. One fact that cannot be refuted is that the numbers of deer have to be kept under control for their own good. Deer breed rapidly and could double their numbers at least every three years. There are about 1,000 on Exmoor at present, which is about right, according to Mr

Scott; too many deer and starvation and disease could result. Apart from this, large numbers of deer would mean their wholesale invasion of cultivated land which would bring the farmers out to protect their crops by indiscriminate shooting, and shooting deer is a job for experts. The keepers in the New Forest carry out their own annual cull, too, shooting from specially constructed high seats scattered round the forest like outsize umpire's chairs. An amateur with a gun runs the risk of wounding rather than killing a deer outright, condemning the animal to a slow and miserable death. The idea of trapping deer is unacceptable to most people. Even Dick Bell, who tried it once when he was young, did not like that.

'Deer poaching sounds romantic, doesn't it?' he said. 'Well, it isn't. We put this snare up one night and the next morning there was a deer caught in it, so one of my mates, a big fellow who looked like Popeye the Sailor Man, he poleaxed it. It was horrible. I'd never do it again.'

Another unpalatable fact is that animals do not regulate their numbers by 'natural wastage'. An old or sick animal is unlikely to die quietly and 'naturally', but will probably be killed by a more powerful member of the herd or die of starvation following an injury. In the end, the realistic choice comes down either to having somebody controlling the deer on Exmoor, or to having no deer on Exmoor.

Exmoor is an area of outstanding natural beauty, wild and haunting and satisfying enough to the eye by any standards. But the idea that, as you scan the heather-covered slopes and coombs, you might be fortunate enough to see red deer, adds an extra thrill to the enjoyment of the scenery. Maurice Scott pointed out that because the local deer are not stalked and shot at as they are in Scotland, they are much more likely to stay out on open ground where people can see them. October is the rutting season for the red deer too. The big stags do not take up a stand like the fallow bucks, but move across the moor with their collection of hinds, ready to fight off any challenge the younger males might make to their authority.

'The rutting season varies,' Maurice Scott said. 'This year it began early. That means we are going to have a mild spring.'

Before I could challenge that piece of folklore, Maurice Scott had stopped the car and was pointing through the windscreen.

'Look,' he said. 'Deer.'

'Where?' I said. I could not see a thing.

'There. Right in front of your eyes. Not 200 yards away. See them?'

'No.'

Sighing with exasperation, Maurice Scott grabbed his field-glasses and got out of the car for a better look. I admired a rainbow that was arching across the sky over Porlock, and then, when I looked back, I saw the deer. Three hinds standing in a row, their dark brown and grey coats merging almost perfectly with the background. They were all standing with their heads up, staring fixedly to their right.

'There must be something down there,' said Maurice, getting back into the car . . . a little further on he stopped the car again and had another look around with his field-glasses.

'There's a magnificent stag over there,' he said. 'I'll drive round to where we can get a better look at him.'

When he stopped the car again, we both got out and looked. Down in the coomb below us there was a stag lying on the ground with his hinds grouped round him, lying dotted about at a respectful distance from the huge, dark-grey shape of the male.

'He's got a wonderful head on him,' Mr Scott said.

His antlers were vast, tipped with white and beautifully symmetrical: it was a sight to remember.

In the rutting season the big stags roar to warn off other males.

'Their necks swell up and they make this thrilling, blood-curdling noise,' Maurice Scott said. 'When you get one on each side of the valley, they really make the place ring. People come out at night just to listen to them.'

The Devon and Somerset Staghounds hunt three days a week from the 1st of August to the end of April. They hunt the old stags betwen August and the third week of October (i.e. stags of five years and over), then they hunt the hinds between November and the end of February, and then the young stags between two and four years old during March and April. Maurice Scott said that they took about 100 deer a year, the numbers working out about equal between stags and hinds. Apart from the sport, the overall aim is to take out any animals which are old, or which have deformed heads (antlers) so that the breed as a whole is improving all the time.

'We cull the old stags at the beginning of the season,' Maurice Scott said. 'They'd be covering their own daughters, else, and that sort of in-breeding could wipe them all out in time. We are proud of our deer here in the West Country because we have such a nice, healthy, good lot.'

On an average hunting day there would be about seventy or eighty riders on horseback and about a hundred cars following the hunt.

'The numbers are increasing all the time,' Maurice Scott told me. 'Anyone can join in if they want to. There's nothing exclusive about it.'

The huntsman will take between fourteen and a half and twenty-one and a half couples of staghounds out, always hunting bitches or dogs; they never hunt them together. A staghound looks like a foxhound and they are bred for the job. Maurice Scott had been out early that morning, helping to exercise the hounds. 'This morning I walked out with sixty couples,' he said. 'There were just the two of us and we walked them for two or three miles, along the road where there were horses, cars and other dogs. Your average townsperson can't take one dog out without a lead and we can take 120 – no trouble at all. That's how obedient they are.'

The idea of a pack of staghounds hunting down an exhausted deer is probably one of the most distasteful images of all. In fact, according to Maurice Scott, the reality is rather different. The pack of hounds are put 'on the line' (the scent) of the stag or hind to be hunted and the hounds hunt by scent, not by sight. They have their noses down 'on the line' and they can follow that line for up to two hours after the deer has gone.

'The hounds spread out and they are "speaking" all the time,' Maurice Scott said. 'You've heard hounds, haven't you? The noise they make is a form of communication between themselves but it also lets the huntsmen know where they are. The huntsmen are riding behind them and if we want to stop them for any reason, we just ride ahead and tell them to "Hold Hard" and they stop. Yes, even when they're hot on the scent, they stop.'

The chase can take anything from half an hour to four hours.

'For the first part of the chase, I would say that the stag enjoys it,' Maurice Scott said. 'I've seen them stop and have a mud bath and let the hounds get right up to them. They know very well that the hounds would never attack them, you see.'

I had imagined that that was exactly what the hounds were for. Maurice Scott tutted impatiently.

'The original purpose of hunting deer was for meat,' he said tersely. 'So it would be ludicrous to allow the hounds to rip the animal to pieces wouldn't it? You'd have nothing left. The hounds are not trained to kill; they are trained to follow the scent of the deer we have selected and to ignore any others. That is bred into them. So, when a stag has tried all the tricks he knows to shake them off, he stands to bay. Another popular misconception is that when a stag stands at bay he is totally exhausted. Not true – he's ready to fight. He looks magnificent, arrogant. He's defying anything to come near him. And, believe me, nothing would attack a stag standing to bay. They are vicious and they could do a lot of damage. The red deer are the biggest of the lot: a stag would be something over twelve hands (four feet) high at the shoulder. When he has been brought to bay, he's shot. He's dead. The hounds never touch him.'

All the animals hunted by the Devon and Somerset staghounds are either shot or get away and Maurice Scott estimated that, over the season, between 50 and 60 per cent of the deer hunted get away.

The culling of stags by the hunt means that for each 'meet' a specific animal, which is considered to be inferior in some way, is chosen to be the quarry. This is the job of the harbourer.

'A harbourer is a very highly respected member of the field,' Maurice Scott said. 'If you're a harbourer, everyone wants to know you on the morning of the meet.'

Harbourers are, in fact, experts on deer. Just as skilled as stalkers, they can tell, by looking at a slot (a footprint), the sex, size and age of the animal that made it. There are no deer keepers on Exmoor: if you want to know about deer, you have to go to the huntsmen or the harbourers.

Maurice Scott took me to meet one of his harbourers, a man called Frank Dallyn, a retired farmer, who had been associated with the hunt for many years and had been acting as harbourer for the last six years. Frank Dallyn is a small man with a kind, round, smiling face and a gentle West Country burr to his voice. To see him sitting by the fire in his cottage, it was difficult to imagine him galloping across the moor on horseback with the hunt, but this is his lifelong liking and his joy. I asked him how he knew where the deer would be and how he selected the deer for the hunt.

'We have a rough idea where they are,' he said. 'And the local farmers keep a watch out for us. I ring round and find out what they have to say. I also ride out on the moor every day, so I know where there are deer. And then the night before a hunt, I go out in the Land Rover and watch where the stags come out to feed, and then, the next morning, I go back again, just as it's getting daylight, to see where they go into cover. There might be a bunch of them together, young and old and maybe two or three eligible ones, so I decide on one and I know that if that one doesn't come out, another will be next in line. I'm looking for one that is right to cull out, you see.

'The worst thing that can happen to me is a really thick early morning fog. It's the most annoying thing for a harbourer because if it's very bad in the morning and then suddenly clears up about ten o'clock, all the people who arrive for the hunt want to know why you haven't a stag laid on for them!

'Another problem is that even if you see exactly where the stags go back into cover, that doesn't mean they will stay there. I will always remember one meet. We saw a stag in the evening and next morning I went back with a friend and we never saw a thing. I was getting edgier and edgier and then one single stag came across the road. It was in the spring and it had a real grotty head on it, but it went under a beech fence and disappeared. That was half past six in the morning. We stayed and stayed and stayed but we saw nothing. I always remember turning up at that meet. All those people there. "God," I thought, "if that stag isn't there, there's nothing else to go for." Lucky enough he was there.' Frank sat back in his armchair and laughed.

The hunt begins with Frank, on horseback, and a few chosen members of the hunt, taking five and a half couples of hounds to the cover where Frank thinks the stag they want is – 'where he *should* be,' said Frank with feeling – to 'tuft' him out.

But how do the dogs know which stag you want, I asked?

'Will you stop calling them dogs?' Maurice Scott said, for the fifth time that day. He covered his eyes in mock despair. 'She keeps calling them dogs,' he told Frank.

'Hounds, *hounds*,' Frank corrected gently.

'There are plenty of people to make sure the hounds get on the line of the right stag,' Maurice Scott said, 'although it can take time. If there are big ones and small ones there, the big stags don't come out first. They send the little ones out. I've actually seen a big stag prong a little one up the backside to get it moving. They are very intelligent animals, you know.'

'I would say that deer are far cleverer than human beings,' Frank said. 'Yes, really. I would stand by that.'

'I remember one day,' Maurice Scott said, nodding in agreement, 'when I was up on the road overlooking the field where the huntsman and the tufters were drawing the cover for a stag. From where I was standing I could see the stag lying down, but the huntsman couldn't. The hounds were actually jumping over him and he never moved a muscle. I told you the hounds hunted by scent didn't I?'

'If a stag has been lying in the same place for a while, there's no lead for the hounds to follow, you see,' Frank said. 'There's no line to him.'

So the scent the hounds follow comes from the feet of the deer, not their bodies, and since the hounds can follow 'a line' for mile after mile and ignore any other deer they come across on the way, each deer must have a scent that is peculiar to that animal.

When the stag selected by the harbourer has finally been singled out, the 'tufters' are stopped and the huntsman blows for the rest of the pack and the field (riders) to join him, and then the whole hunt moves off. The harbourer's job is finished.

'You could go home then?' I said to Frank.

'I could, but I don't,' he replied, smiling.

'If the deer were in a state of terror when the hounds got on their scent, you would expect them to run away as fast as they could in a straight line, wouldn't you?' Maurice Scott said. 'But they don't. They make use of livestock – sheep and so on. They run through them to confuse the hounds, they do U-turns, they use the rivers;

they are full of tricks and it is only when they have used up all their tricks that they stand at bay.

'Nobody likes killing them. I don't like to see a dead stag, but we have to cull them to keep the species healthy and thriving. At the same time I am not saying for one moment that there is not a tremendous satisfaction in galloping across the moor behind a pack of hounds.'

'I was standing by a farm drive once,' Frank said, 'and a hind came up the drive, jumped over the fence into a field and went right round the field twice, two complete circles. Then she turned round and retraced her steps, slot for slot (footprint for footprint), and popped back over the fence again. When the hounds came into the field they were completely lost. I would not have believed it if I hadn't seen it with my own eyes.'

A few years ago the Devon Trust for Nature Conservation carried out an independent survey on the red deer of Exmoor. They concluded that the indiscriminate control of deer by a minority of private landowners was not justified and that ideally culling should only be performed under the auspices of an official organisation. They further found that 'the pressure against organised hunting practices with hounds' is the most serious immediate threat to the continued successful existence of red deer on Exmoor. They also stated:

> *It is important to appreciate the nature of culling deer with hounds and the importance of the hunt within the community that currently successfully integrates the activities of farmers, foresters and a wealth of people enjoying Exmoor.*

Ministry of Agriculture regulations state that all sheep must be dipped twice a year, once between June and the beginning of August and again between the end of September and the beginning of November, to prevent sheep scab. Any large-scale movement of sheep at this time of year means that the farmers are rounding up their flocks for the second dip.

Harry Ridley manages a 1,700 acre farm near Winchester in Hampshire. He was born in Durham and sounds more like a hill sheep man than the downland farmer that he is. In fact, he stands at the opposite end of the sheep production line from the upland farmer. His stock originates on the upland grazing farms, bred by people like Willie Parker in Hexham, Northumberland. Harry Ridley knows Willie Parker well . . .

'Everyone knows Willie Parker, don't they?'

The sheep that Willie Parker breeds for himself are pure Swaledale, but those he breeds for selling south are Swaledale ewes crossed with a Blue-Faced Leicester ram to produce Mules.

'Mules are prolific breeders and good milkers, but they still have the hardiness in them which suits our system here because we lamb outside and the Mules suit us for finishing on grass,' Harry Ridley said. 'I look on the whole country as one big farm,' he continued. 'And you do with your land what it will best do. Because people like Willie Parker live high up, they breed a hardy sheep that live on the mountains and eat heather and grass, and they put a ram onto that which produces a sheep that comes down to the lowlands.

'We are each dependent on the other. We buy the breeding sheep from them. They are the breeders of stock and we buy the females from them; if our market collapses at this end and we stop buying, then their market collapses. We like stock from up there because they have hybrid vigour – lambs that can get up and go, 'livability'. They've had this bred into them over generations. We buy them, put a ram with them and produce a lamb that gives us the right sort of carcase, the sort that people are demanding these days. On this particular farm we buy shearlings (one and a half years old and sheared once) and go straight into production. Other people, like my son on his farm for instance, will buy younger stock, get a lamb off them in spring and then sell them on to people like us.'

The popularity of the Mules means that there are now all sorts of Mules – Blue-Faced Leicester rams have been crossed with Scottish Black-faced sheep, Beulahs and Welsh Speckle-Faced Mountain Sheep.

'I would say there were more Mules in the South of England now than anything else,' Harry Ridley said. 'You have to be careful what you're getting nowadays. What I'm after are the Swale Mules.'

Harry Ridley is a small, grey-haired man with a slightly diffident manner, but behind his quiet, modest exterior lies a sharp, clear mind. Harry is a great man for getting farming into perspective and poking gentle fun at himself and his colleagues. He goes up to the markets in the North of England with his son every year to buy stock.

'When we go to the sales, all the stock there is sold as "good stock off high land" – "Grand Shifting Gimmers" they call them, "good lively sheep". We interpret that as meaning anything with three legs from anywhere six inches above sea-level. (A gimmer is a young, female sheep.)

'At the market there are also the strong lambs that will go to the tup this year and the smaller ones we call the "runners" that will not be bred from until the following year,' he said. 'And then there are the very poor lambs that you can buy cheap, but you can't get pigeons out of crows, (that's one of Willie's sayings), so we don't waste our money on them.'

From his shearlings, Harry Ridley expects a good lambing rate. He says that he is not interested in litters, that two lambs to a sheep suit him nicely.

'But as you know,' he said, 'the favourite pastime for any sheep is to die . . . and the same goes for the lambs. You must have seen a newly-born lamb that looks and acts as if it's in league with the undertaker? Given a bit of warmth and care it should be able to stand up – you know the performance, all four legs on the same spot. Then comes the waltzing, followed by the splits, and finally you know you have succeeded when it piddles on the carpet. Apart from all these troubles, there's no reason why you should not end up with a 200 per cent lambing rate – or at least claim it – everyone else does.

'Any flock of sheep will include the jumpers, the thinkers and the lie-down-and-die brigade.

'The cure is simple,' Harry went on. 'Send the jumpers back, shoot the thinkers and ring up the kennels for the lie-down-and-diers.' He shot me a quick, sideways glance to make sure I wasn't taking all this too seriously. 'They always say a shepherd's favourite tool is a spade,' said Harry. 'He can either use it to bury them with or he can hit them with it, straight between the ears.'

In the twenty-two years Harry Ridley has been at the farm, it has become a smooth-running, totally integrated system under his management, growing corn and grazing three thousand ewes. In his opinion the two enterprises are totally complementary. The land goes through a seven-year rotation – two years' grass, one year peas (to restore nitrogen to the soil), two years' winter wheat and one year winter barley, and in the seventh year spring barley is undersown with grass so that the land reverts back to grazing.

'You could say we use sheep as the break crop if you like,' he said. 'And of course sheep manure is "warm" muck and there's nothing like it for the land. They spread it around as they go, you see. It's not like cows, dropping great platters of the stuff, usually just where you don't want it.'

I said that a pig farmer had told me that there was nothing better for grass than pig muck.

'Well, he would say that wouldn't he?' Harry Ridley said, 'being a pig farmer. No, sheep muck is best. If you ever want to grow sweet peas, get hold of some and try it. It grows beautiful sweet peas.'

Apart from the natural fertiliser supplied by the sheep, Harry Ridley treats the land with nitrogen. . . .

'You know what they call that up north, don't you?' he said. 'Electric shit.'

Because there are so many sheep to be dipped, Harry Ridley and his shepherd find it easier to take a mobile dip to the flocks rather than bring all the sheep back to the farm. Driving to the dip we passed a piece of land overgrown with scrub.

'They said that thirteen-acre site was "of special scientific interest",' Harry Ridley said. 'So they asked me not to graze it. That was ten years ago, and look at it now. There are supposed to be some sort of rare orchids in there and a special moth or something of that sort. Now they've asked me to put the sheep in again to clear it up, but I have refused. I told them: "You need sheep that can climb trees for that lot and I haven't any of those." '

We arrived at the mobile sheep dip. A wooden open pen, a wooden crush pen, a metal 'race' (a long passage one sheep wide) and a steep ramp led up to a platform which contained the dip, One man was standing on the platform and pulling the sheep, sideways, into the dip as they reached the top of the ramp. Three more men and three dogs were manœuvring the sheep from one pen to the next, along the race and up the ramp. The sheep did not want to go.

'It's the smell they remember,' Harry said. 'The first time they're dipped they will trot up quite happily, but after that, they'll do their best to avoid going in. We have two sheep at the top there, decoy sheep, just standing on the platform, so the other sheep will see them and follow them up, because that is the nature of sheep, to follow one another. Do you know that in New Zealand in the abattoirs they have what they call "Judas sheep"? They're tame sheep they keep there just to bring the others in.'

It was hard, physical work for all the men, hauling the reluctant sheep along the race and up the ramp, and especially hard work for John, at the top, pulling them in, ducking them under the sharp-smelling dip and helping them out at the other end. The dip he was using was about eight feet long, with a slope out at the far end. When John the Baptist had finished immersing his flock (one minute each and one complete submersion), he descended from his platform and spake unto me. He turned out to be John Read, Head Shepherd, and selected as Shepherd of the Year in a national competition in 1981.

'Ewes,' he said. 'They're more intelligent than most of the people who work with them.' His assistants laughed sheepishly while John Read went on. 'Sheep have defined ways of thinking; they are flock animals so in a group they feel secure. It is when you have to take one out of the group that the problems arise.

'The art of moving sheep about is based on the fact that they will stay in a mob. Once you've got them together you can go for miles with them. They have their own social order in the flock and some sheep are leaders, just like humans. You get the same ones turning up at the front of the flock every time. With young sheep, before they have got themselves sorted out and a leader has emerged, it's more difficult. They keep going round and round in circles. The only way to get over that is to put a couple of old ewes in with them to lead.

'Sheep are quite good swimmers, you know, but they don't like water at all. I suppose that's because, down the years, the ones that did like water drowned.' He laughed and pulled his cap down over his eyes. 'But seriously though,' he said, 'if it had rained hard and there was a pool of water in the path a herd of cows would walk straight through it, but a flock of sheep would split up to go round it – following one another. They'll do anything to avoid water.

'The instinct to follow has helped sheep to survive: those that did not stay with the flock perished. When you work with them you have to use these instincts, not try to work against them. The only time I've known the instinct to follow to become a problem was when we put about six or seven hundred sheep out in a field which had a square wood in it, about a hundred yards square. The sheep started walking round the wood. When they got to a corner, they'd catch sight of other sheep disappearing round the next corner and follow them and so on. We had to go out and break them up in the end.

'The longer I work with sheep,' he said, smiling, 'the more like human beings they seem to me. I notice it more and more. It frightens me sometimes.'

Immediately after dipping, most farmers will be sorting our their flocks, prior to tupping. If the lambs are to arrive in the following April, it is time to put the rams in with the ewes.

Andrew Jones, on his farm near Lampeter in West Wales, looks forward eagerly to this opportunity to study his sheep and to decide exactly which ewes to put with which rams.

'I want to do better every year, see,' he explained. 'It's not a case of keeping up with the Joneses, it's for my own satisfaction. Whatever I did this year, I want to do better next year.'

Standing looking at his ewes, Andrew Jones is weighing up all the possibilities. He carries a little notebook in his shirt pocket in which he has written down all he needs to know about each ewe.

'See that one there, P34?' he said, consulting the book. 'She's lambed twice, four lambs once and triplets once. She's strong and hardy: I'll breed from her. Now that one, over there, she's a very common sort of ewe – no body, too short and condensed. I don't like short ewes myself. Her mother was longer, so obviously the ram didn't click there. That one by the fence, P40 – she's a good ewe: very alert, nice black head. I could spend all day just watching them, you know.

'It's a challenge, see, to put the right ewes and rams together to produce lambs that will have a bigger frame to work on before they get too fat. This breeding business is engrossing. Over the last four years the anti-fat campaign has been gathering strength. The lambs we were producing five years ago wouldn't do now.'

Andrew Jones will be putting fourteen rams in with the flock and keeping three or four in reserve. Just before tupping time he keeps all the rams together in the barn so they get used to one another and will be less likely to fight when they are turned out with the ewes.

'In September we feed the ewes up before we put the rams in and we also feed the rams well so they will be really strong,' he said. 'We keep the rams inside – that's the safest. If they were in an adjoining field, they would be hopping over the hedge to get to the ewes. You can't trust them, they won't listen. Then, just before we put the rams in we "dag" the ewes, which means cleaning them up and shearing their tails, because some of the rams will be working so hard at tupping time that we have to make it easier for them. We don't want any mishaps.'

If Andrew Jones thinks a ram is getting a bit too complacent with his ewes, he will put a ram lamb into the field with him, because the youngster will serve as a threat and the ram will 'buck his ideas up a bit'. The three or four reserve rams are kept back for about a month and then Andrew puts them in with the ewes because, after about four weeks, 'the rams begin to lose momentum'.

The rams are a mixed bunch to provide different lambs for different purposes. There are pure-bred ones, Texel ones and the Blue-Faced Leicester rams to produce Welsh Mules, although, according to Andrew, some of the older farmers think that 'putting a Blue-Faced Leicester to a traditional Welsh Mountain sheep is an insult to the sheep'.

'Buying a new ram is the most exciting thing,' said Andrew

Jones. 'I get intense pleasure out of selecting the one I want. I spend the whole day weighing up the rams and picking out the best ones. With a new ram, you've something to look forward to: next spring I'll be watching as the lambs drop, looking to see what they're like. It's a dab of new blood, see? And then, when I've bought the ram and got him home, I get up the next morning and the first thing I do, I go and have another look at him and I think to myself: "Damn, that's a good ram, isn't it?" '

NOVEMBER

When the sun shines in the woods in November, the tall trees look like legendary kings crowned with gold, offering themselves as sacrificial victims to the dark gods of winter. Soon the glory will be gone, but the seeds of the future have been sown. Next year's buds are already on the branches and even the catkins are hanging from the hazel trees, cocooned in green, preparing for the time when they will emerge to lead the dance into spring. The King is dead. Long live the King!

The New Forest in Hampshire had been a royal hunting forest long before William the Conqueror arrived in England and declared it 'My New Forest' in about 1079. The forest today forms an unbroken link with the past; the same ground, the same types of ancient woodland, the same late-autumn covering of tawny leaves stretching away into the distance. Driving through the Forest with an elderly keeper employed by the Forestry Commission, I longed for a quick flashback: just a glimpse of a royal hunting party in pursuit of the hind or the wild boar. The keeper stopped the van because he thought he had seen something moving about among the trees. We walked into the forest and suddenly a huge saddleback boar came trotting briskly out towards us, snuffling as it ran. We raced back to the van and the keeper drove to the nearest cottage where a young woman was standing in the garden.

'Your boar's out,' he called to her.

'Oh no!' she said. 'Isn't he naughty? I'll go and get him back.'

'Quiet, is he?'

'Like a little lamb,' she said, smiling, and strolled off down the forest path to collect him.

'They can be very nasty, you know,' the keeper said, not at all amused, 'Very vicious.'

When William I transformed the New Forest into an official

hunting preserve, the peasants were forbidden to enclose their land, so they were allowed to graze their domestic animals in the forest. About 5,000 animals now graze the open forest: ponies, cattle, sheep and pigs. The pigs are turned out during the 'Pannage Season' when the acorns and beechmast provide food for them . . . all except the boars, that is, who are supposed to stay at home.

By the Middle Ages the grazing by common right had resulted in a serious shortage of trees, so a Tree Growing Act was passed in 1482, enabling large areas of the forest to be enclosed for the growing of timber, fenced off to protect the young trees from any damage caused by animals. By the end of the sixteenth century the foresters began to share a place of equal importance with the keepers. An account of tree-planting in the seventeenth century records that oak trees were sown, rather than planted as they are today: 'Half a bushel of acorns was allotted for each forest worker to plant in a day. Three acorns were sown in each bed or spit and the spits were spaced a yard apart.' Nobody in the Forestry Department in the Forestry Commission Headquarters at Brockenhurst was quite sure how many acorns would fit into half a bushel, so comparison was difficult, but one of the foresters, Paul Barwick, told me that a forest worker today would be expected to plant something like 500 oak trees a day. The trees to be planted in the New Forest come from the Forestry Commission nurseries where they are grown to a height of about six or twelve inches, and arrive either bare-rooted or, preferably, in pots.

'Once a tree is lifted out of the ground, it goes into a state of shock. It goes dormant and the roots stop growing,' Paul Barwick said, adding that trees are a great deal more sensitive in early life than is generally supposed. 'Bare-rooted trees come in bags of a hundred,' he continued, 'and if some idiot drops a bag, some of those trees will die straight away.'

Oak trees are normally planted close together because, even in pots, some will not survive. The density of a plantation depends to some extent on the shape of timber the forester is looking for when the tree has grown.

'If you plant one tree by itself, it will take the line of least resistance,' Paul Barwick said. 'It has all the nutrients and all the light it needs, so it will grow outwards. If you plant a lot of trees together, the only place they can go is up.'

The forester's plans for his plantation depend, therefore, on whether he wants short thick trees or tall thin ones.

'But the fascinating thing is that whatever shape the trees are, you will end up with the same *volume* of timber,' Paul said.

Out in the plantations with Paul Barwick it was noticeable that, even in November, the oak trees still had a good covering of leaves.

'They are among the last trees to shed their leaves because they come into leaf twice a year,' Paul told me. 'The oak trees have evolved this second "flushing" because, of all the trees, the oak has the most insect parasites. The second flushing in August, the "Lammas growth", replaces the leaves lost to the insects since April.'

But even in a group of trees of the same species, some were losing their leaves faster than others. Did that mean they were dying? Not necessarily. Paul explained that it was probably because of their provenance (literally 'the fact of coming from some particular source or quarter') or, in other words, because their parents probably came from a warmer climate, so they were less resistant to the cold and they shed earlier.

The remaining leaves hung from the branches, in rich translucent veils of colour, facing winter's coming with graceful acquiescence.

> . . .I will hold
> Out my worn dress for dread
> Winter's unweaving
> In the cold.

> (Elizabeth Daryush)

The North Norfolk coast is one of England's most beautiful and unspoilt coastlines, made up of ever-changing sand-flats, shingle ridges, spits and dunes – the perfect place to attract such winter migrants as brent geese, pink-footed geese and wigeon. Joe Reed, National Trust Warden, drove me down from Cley Village towards Morston Harbour.

'We'll have a run down to Blakeney Point and see what's there,' he said.

He stopped the car and walked over to a boat. We were going by boat. Another boat, but a small one this time with an outboard motor.

We started with a roar and zoomed off across the water, banging down hard into each trough between the waves, making for the open sea and the tip of the long sandy spit that is Blakeney Point. There seemed to be an unlimited amount of water about, and of sky. Cormorants stood on a sand-bank and then took off as we approached, but the brent geese were more tolerant, just lifting their black heads like a forest of miniature periscopes, to watch us as we passed. Near the end of Blakeney Point there were seals swimming all around us, round heads appearing in the water, huge dark eyes watching us gravely. Joe said that most of the seals were common seals, but there were about fifteen to twenty grey seals amongst them. The largest number of seals congregate in the area around July when there will be well over 500 of them, made up of both adults and pups of up to five years old.

'We leave the seals pretty much to look after themselves,' Joe said. 'They will tolerate a good deal of disturbance.'

The intertidal mud-flats at Blakeney Point are completely natural and the formation of the sand-dunes changes constantly with the winds and the tides. The reserve attracts something like 60,000 visitors a year and Joe Reed's job is to maintain a balance between the recreational use of the area and preservation, monitoring the situation carefully and taking any steps necessary to protect the wild birds and their fragile habitats.

Every year Joe Reed and his assistants go out and count all the breeding birds in his area, a coordinated count with everyone out at the same time so that they arrive at a reasonably accurate figure, and in November Joe is busy preparing his annual report which will include a list of every bird seen in the area during the year. The sandwich terns are the first breeding birds to arrive; they come in in March and can build up to as many as 4,000 pairs. There will also be about 300 pairs of common terns and 160 pairs of the much rarer little terns.

'That's the largest single colony of little terns in the whole of Western Europe,' Joe Reed said.

In late September and October the geese will start arriving for the winter, geese and ducks.

'You can often hear the geese flying in before you can see them,' Joe Reed said. 'Brent geese are very vocal. You have to experience the noise to explain it. And the ducks too: take wigeon for instance, you would expect them to quack, being ducks. They don't, though, they whistle. Golden-eye ducks you can tell because of the whirr of their wings. If it's light, you can generally tell what the birds are just by where they are in the sky. A truly wild greylag goose would be about four gunshots' high – those true wild geese are very cautious. I can see a flight of birds coming,' Joe Reed said, 'and even when they are half a mile away I can tell you what they are. I can't explain how I know, but I do know. I am always right.'

Brent geese were almost an endangered species twenty-five years ago, but now their numbers have built up and, in a harsh winter, they can be a problem to the farmers in the area, because they move on to the wheat and barley to feed.

'Some farmers and shooting enthusiasts are now proposing that they should be put back on the shooting list,' Joe said, 'but I don't agree. They breed in Siberia and if, for some reason, the ice doesn't clear until late in the season, they just don't breed. They either have a very successful year or a complete failure. There seems to be nothing in between.'

Joe Reed is a shooting man himself, as well as being a keen photographer.

'I can only justify combining wild-fowling and photography by telling you the truth, which is that I enjoy both of them. At the end of the day I would be sorry if shooting was abolished; I suppose it is in my blood. My grandfather used to make his living from wild-fowling. But it's fieldcraft that gets you close enough to be in the right position for a shot, whether it's with a gun or a camera.'

Joe Reed feels that many people are strangely selective in their attitudes towards the preservation of wild life. 'Of course there's some cruelty in wild-fowling,' he said, 'but people don't always think about the cruelty involved in other things. They drive up here and look at the birds and criticise the wild-fowlers, but they don't for a moment stop to think of the damage done to the birds from the oil-slicks on the sea which wouldn't be there if these people didn't demand petrol for their cars.'

Another local man emphasised this point as he talked about the number of birds found affected by oil which were brought to him for cleaning-up.

'The birds swallow the oil, you know. They try and clean themselves and the oil gets into their throats and burns them; they must suffer a great deal. I wonder whether, in the end, it wouldn't be kinder to put them out of their misery straight away. People these days are more interested in the quantity of life than the quality, but I don't agree. I'm old-fashioned.'

Joe Reed turned the boat round and headed back for the shore.

'Brent geese on your left, pintails to your right,' he yelled, over the noise of the engine.

The sky had darkened to purple-grey over the land and the sun, covered by cloud, cast a long, narrow path of light over the surface of the water, a silver swathe shining like silk. Joe sat relaxed in the stern of the boat, whistling as he steered. Two huge birds flew low across the silvery light – black-backed gulls according to Joe, who was smiling with pleasure. I could understand his passionate attachment to the place.

The Cley Marsh Nature Reserve was the first County Trust Reserve to be set up in this country, founded in 1926 by a Norwich man, Dr Sidney Long, who bought the Cley marshes and founded the Norfolk Naturalists' Trust, with the object of administering the reserve, conserving the wildlife of the area and attracting rare species of birds by improving the habitat. Cley Marsh is a fresh-water marsh, reclaimed from salt water. It was officially designated a Bird Sanctuary in 1966. Bernard Bishop is Warden of the Reserve, the third generation of his family to hold that position.

'You can please some of the people some of the time,' he said, 'but there are those who think that everything should be left totally natural. Now, this reserve has been interfered with from the start, and we're improving it all the time – encouraging the reeds to grow and creating new "scrapes" (shallow pools for the waders) – and once you've started interfering, you have to keep it up.'

As Joe Reed had said:

'The days have gone when you could say that nature will take its own course,' he had said. 'Wild life today has to be managed. At last we are opening our eyes to how much damage has been done in the past, and it is up to us to do something about it.'

'I don't see how you can create a habitat and encourage the birds to nest and not try to control the vermin,' Bernard Bishop said. 'I'm not saying you should kill the last one, but they have to be controlled.'

Bernard Bishop still lives in Watcher's Cottage where he was born. Bernard Bishop's father, Billy, had been an expert, with an unrivalled eye and 'feel for birds'; he had been a colourful character whose wisdom and no-nonsense approach were relished by all those who knew him, and the improvements he carried out to the marsh attracted three rarities back to the area, the avocets, the bearded reedlings and the bitterns. Now the Cley Marsh Reserve has one of the largest colonies of avocets breeding in this country.

'I used to go out on the reserve with my father and help him,' Bernard said. 'It was a lovely childhood.'

Sitting at the kitchen table, drinking tea with Bernard Bishop we looked out over the reserve.

'It is never the same twice,' he said. 'You get different lights on the reeds all the time and the water-levels change all through the winter. In winter I feel as if the marsh belongs to me. We start cutting the reeds just before Christmas and sell them to the thatchers. Those reeds are a beautiful green in summer and then when the leaves come off they turn a lovely, golden colour.'

'We get mostly migratory waders here.' Bernard Bishop said. 'We get long-legged birds like sandpipers, red-shanks, green-shanks and various stints, and we get the occasional surprise. Last year a little whimbrel turned up. They're supposed to migrate from Japan to Australia so I don't know what it was doing here. We had a Rosser's gull too, from the Arctic Circle – a beautiful rose-pink gull. That was a rarity. In March you get the birds nesting – bitterns, bearded reedlings and last year we had 54 pairs of avocets.

It's a mecca for bird-watchers, this place. It's *the* mecca,' he said. 'If you ask anybody interested in birds, they'll tell you that Cley has international status as a reserve.'

I asked him about the reserves in Suffolk, ones like the Minsmere Bird Reserve. He sat back and stared at me blankly.

'Never heard of it,' he said. Going on with an absolutely straight face, he said, 'There's no such place in Suffolk. That's South Norfolk you're talking about.

'I do a bit of wild-fowling at this time of year,' he said. 'There's no conflict – I don't shoot any rare birds and I don't shoot anything I can't eat. I hope to God these fanatical people who don't know what they're talking about and don't understand the countryside don't go and mess everything up. There is a pheasant shoot near here which has just been closed down. The keeper is a friend of mine and I know for a fact how many foxes he had to deal with during the year. What's going to happen to all those foxes now? They're going to come onto the reserve, aren't they? They're not going to go the other way because the bloody things can't swim.'

Bernard stared out of the window at the Marsh again.

'This is where I like to be,' he said. 'God created all this and I'm thankful that there are places like it. I feel so much for the place. I just want to do my best to keep up its reputation.'

Back at the salt marshes in front of Cley Village the sun was setting and an arrow formation of geese was flying out from the land, high above the flocks of starlings which were sweeping over the marsh, mingling and separating in swift, silent streams, as if their very lives depended on one last stunning display before the light left the sky.

'Poaching is not dying out – far from it,' Bob Carter said. By November the poachers are out after pheasants because with most of the leaves off the trees it is much easier to see them roosting, silhouetted against the sky. From November, right through until

February the keeper has to be on duty night and day to protect his birds.

'You can get the odd local who fancies a pheasant for his Sunday dinner, and that's one problem. I like to discourage them,' he said. 'But you can also get groups of people moving into the area who are after as many birds as possible and they can be dangerous. In the old days if you caught somebody red-handed they would come quietly, but not now. You could be in for the beating of your life, if not something worse, if you're not careful.'

Poachers used to be known as 'the sportsmen of the night', but armed and organised gangs are no sportsmen. One advantage the keeper has is that news of a strange car or van parked in the area travels fast. The more out of the way the place where an unfamiliar vehicle is left, the more noticeable it is to local eyes. Warned of possible intruders, the keeper makes his way to the woods, and then, apparently, 'All you have to do then, is listen.'

Sound travels with eerie clarity at night in the country and anybody unfamiliar with the ground will soon give themselves away.

'It can be very dark in the woods at two o'clock in the morning, but I know every inch of the ground and I can move about without making a sound, even though I'm a big fellow,' Bob said. 'The point is that if there is someone in there with a gun, you don't want him to be aware of you until you're right on top of him. I like to come up behind them and tap them on the shoulder.'

The solid darkness of night in the country when there is no moon comes as a shock unless you have been brought up with it. No wonder that poachers, especially those who don't know the area, prefer a moonlit night. 'It's my delight on a shining night in the season of the year', goes the old Poacher's Song. But even the moon can make an uneasy companion. As Ian Niall wrote in his book, *Fresh Woods*: 'The bit of moon comes sailing out of the darkness, a candle carried by some sure-footed, hurrying witch.' Any breeze and the bare tops of the trees scrape together with a noise like a rusty gibbet, and shadows lump together where no shadows should be while the undergrowth stirs with small restless movements.

'I think some of the gangs we get in after the pheasants are scared

181

of the dark,' said Bob. 'I swear I've seen some of them holding hands.' He gave a short laugh. 'It's no good if you're frightened,' he said. 'The only time I've had a scare was one night in November. I was moving quietly along when, about fifteen feet behind me, a vixen screamed. That's a blood-curdling sound at the best of times. It sounds like somebody being murdered. I don't think the hairs on the back of my neck lay down for a week.'

Taking a rabbit for the pot was a traditional country pastime. Myxomatosis decimated the rabbit population in the 1950s, but since then the numbers of farm-workers have steadily decreased and the numbers of rabbits have slowly increased. Rabbits have to be controlled, sometimes with the keeper's blessing and sometimes without.

'Some of the people they bring in to kill rabbits are just cow-boys,' the keeper said in disgust. 'They drive in at night in their vans with the headlights blazing and they blast away. They're not killing rabbits; they're educating them.'

Dick Bell, the odd-job man, enjoys a night out with the keeper, shooting rabbits.

'They're at their prime at this time of year,' he said. 'You need a dark night, no moon and preferably a bit rough. When you pick them up in the headlights you have to put your foot down hard and really move, and when you are ready to shoot, stop. I don't care what anybody says. You can't shoot a rabbit from a moving van.'

Dick Bell and the keeper also go out after rabbits in the daytime with a couple of ferrets.

'The old boys doing a bit of poaching with their ferrets will net up the rabbit holes,' said Dick, 'but we just put the ferrets in and stand back where we can shoot the rabbits as they pop out.'

In *Fresh Woods* Ian Niall writes about the phenomenon of a rabbit which was being hunted by a stoat and which didn't even try to get away: 'Some gland has operated perhaps. The power to run has gone. . . . It began to die back there in the burrow when that strange thing happened to its muscles and its will to escape.' Had Dick Bell ever seen anything like that when he was ferreting?

'Yes, there was a rabbit once that just sat there instead of making a bolt for it.'

'Why do you think it did that?'

'Don't ask me. Maybe it was depressed.'

The trouble with ferrets is that if they are not well behaved they lie up inside the rabbit warrens instead of coming out again, causing their owners a great deal of aggravation and hard work because they have to dig them out. In *The Amateur Poacher*, Richard Jefferies remarked that: 'This digging is very tedious; especially if it is a large warren and you are not sure where to start.'

'The keeper has all the modern technology,' Dick Bell explained. 'He has a bleeper on his ferrets and if one of them lies up, he can pin-point it, straight away, so he knows exactly where to dig.'

Apart from putting a bleeping ferret down the hole, game-keepers and poachers will sometimes snare rabbits on a rabbit run. And what does a rabbit run look like? We went to a field surrounded by woods – 'a good place for rabbits' according to Dick. Sur-rounded by tired old grass and a few dead nettles, it was hard to believe there was anything there to see. There were certainly no rabbits about, but when we got right down and looked at the grass, a network of little pathways leading from the woods soon became visible. The pathways, curving round tussocks of grass, dividing and re-forming, had been travelled constantly by rabbits and the grass was flattened by their feet.

'The rabbits don't just run about anywhere,' Dick said. 'They always follow the same paths, you see.'

So you would put a snare on one of those pathways?

'Not just anywhere,' he said. 'If you watch rabbits moving about, you'll see that they walk for a bit and then they give a hop. What you're looking for is a place where they hop.'

Do they always hop in the same places?

'Look at the grass. It's all panned down for a stretch and then there are a few inches where it's not flattened, where there's a tuft of something growing. That's where they'll hop and if you put your snare there, they'll hop straight into it.'

Dick Bell's small brown dog is an expert rabbiter, but he had left her shut up in the Land Rover just in case there was a stray pheasant in the field. It was a great disappointment for the dog and a real sacrifice on Dick's part because the dog suffers from chronic flatulence and the Land Rover smelt like a sewer. But pheasants are sacred. Pheasants are for the shoot.

At half-past nine on a showery, blustery November morning the syndicate meets to shoot some pheasants. Very few estates can afford to keep the shooting private these days, so they sell off the shooting rights to a group of people who each pay around £2,500 for fourteen days' shooting a year. Some big estates boast about bagging something like 1,800 birds in one day.

'I call that slaughter,' Bob Carter said. 'If you have enough money you can buy yourself a day's shooting on some estates, but that's for people with money to burn. And believe me, some of those people couldn't hit a barn if they were standing in it.'

The syndicate on this 2,000 acre estate is more traditional. Today there are ten guns who all meet regularly for the shooting. The head of the syndicate organises the guns and pays the keeper's wages. Everything is prepared for them. The keeper arrives with twenty beaters, hired for the day, and leads the guns to their positions, marked by numbered stakes spread out across a field between two woods. The guns have already picked numbers out of a hat to decide which position they will take up for the first drive. Between each of the six drives of the day they will move up two numbers so that each gun gets his fair share of the best positions.

Meanwhile the beaters have moved off to the far side of the wood on top of the hill. The keeper has been feeding the pheasants in that wood every day, but at night the birds return to the wood behind the guns to roost. The idea is that once the beaters start disturbing them, the pheasants will fly over the guns.

'They will want to go home once the shooting starts,' Bob Carter explained.

When everyone is in position there is a whistle from the keeper to signal that the beaters have started, and the guns concentrate their attention on the wood in front of them. Suddenly a cock pheasant flies out but then crumples in the air and drops onto the field like a feathery thunderbolt. Only when the bird hits the ground does the sound of the shot reach our ears. The delay gives the sudden incident an unreal quality.

184

Standing behind the guns is Dick Bell, whose job is to watch where the birds fall so they can be picked up later. He is a crack shot himself but, on a shoot like this, he explains, 'It's them and us'.

'I just hope that when these gentlemen shoot behind, they shoot high,' he says gloomily. He points to one of the syndicate. 'See that gun he's got there? That's a Hudson and Hudson. A pair of those would cost you twenty-five thousand pounds.'

The beaters can be heard from the wood ahead, shouting and hollering and whistling as they come. Dick has done his share of beating in his time.

'You have to keep in a straight line, right through the brambles and everything, otherwise you get sworn at from all directions,' he said. 'The idea is to send the birds over in waves to give the guns a chance. If all the birds came out at once there would be one big blast and that would be it.'

(The twelve-bore shot-guns carried by the members of the syndicate can only fire twice before they have to be reloaded.)

A wave of pheasants fly out and the guns blast away in vain.

'Oh dear, dear, dear,' Dick Bell mutters in disgust. 'You've got to keep swinging. When you pick a bird up in front of the barrel, you must swing round as it flies and when you pull the trigger, keep on swinging because if the gun stops moving you are going to miss. Like the old men always say, "Don't poke 'em, stroke 'em".'

A hen pheasant bustles into the undergrowth. She has just run down the whole length of the field and the guns could not touch her: no bird can be shot when it is on the ground, and no bird can be shot if it is flying too low. It is not done to blow a bird to pieces. Neither should you shoot a bird that is flying too high because there is a danger you might just 'prick' it instead of killing it outright. (You cannot shoot any pheasants at all on a Sunday because pheasants are 'game' and it is against the law to shoot game on a Sunday, although you can shoot vermin on a Sunday – and the logic behind all that is beyond me.)

Another wave of birds.

'Well, at least Bob has done his job,' Dick says. 'He's shown the birds.'

The guns get a few and Dick watches where they fall. One will not take any finding at all; it whistles down and would have dropped on Dick's head if he had not stepped aside just in time. The birds that reach the wood behind the guns drift down into the trees making chuckling sounds as they glide in.

There is another whistle from the keeper and the beaters appear from the wood. The first drive of the day is over. Dick Bell picks up the dead pheasants and takes them to the Land Rover where he sorts them into braces (one male and one female).

'No, of course you don't get exactly equal numbers of male and female, don't be silly.'

'What do you think, Dick?' says Bob Carter as he passes by.

Dick shakes his head in dismay.

'Pathetic,' Bob agrees. 'The birds are too good for them.'

While we are waiting in the Land Rover for the shoot to move on to the next drive, one of the syndicate comes up.

'How many have we got, Dick?'

'About thirty-five, sir.'

'That wind do lift 'em. Just as you're going to pull, they shoot up a couple of yards.'

'Mmm,' Dick says diplomatically.

There are plenty of birds left for another day and the white pheasant that only Bob and Dick know about has been left undisturbed.

> His face is pale and shrunk, his shining hair
> Is prison-shorn;
> Trailing his grey cloak, up the short dark stair
> He creeps each morn.
> Looks out to his lost throne, to the noon-height
> Once his, then turns
> Back to the alien dungeon, where all night
> Unseen he burns.
>
> (Elizabeth Daryush, *November Sun*)

DECEMBER

The colour is draining out of the countryside. The extravagant reds and golds of autumn have gone, leaving a simplicity of empty fields and bare trees. The fields lie under their heavy winter blanket of dark earth, some under the brown quilted hummocks of newly turned soil, some with a sprinkling of green where the autumn-sown crops are showing.

Underfoot in the woods the rich carpet of fallen leaves is fading now, darkened and sodden after the rain, but the bracken has turned to the colour of new leather. Surrounding the dark shapes of the evergreens, the trunks and branches of the trees shine with a watery blue-green light where the rain has accentuated the underwater tones of the algae and lichen.

> *Come into the woods*
> *see the wonder-change;*
> *On everything broods*
> *a beauty strange. . . .*
>
> *when the heavens are dank*
> *The lands icy,*
> *earth is on the brink*
> *Of a mystery. . . .*

(Elizabeth Daryush, *Modern Carol*)

From a distance the woods are a tweedy mixture of soft colours, but it is the shape of the bare trees that draws the eye. Instead of the moving blocks of colour of summer, there is a motionless engraving, framed between earth and sky. The slanting, pale sun turns the wet roads and water-filled tracks to silver. There is a shining and a hardness about the look of the landscape. The frost is coming and maybe the snow.

It is hard weather for Ivan Swaile, the fisher of men, to venture out in the night in search of salmon poachers on the River Tyne in Northumberland. By November the salmon will have completed their long, arduous journey to their spawning grounds and the riverheads are the lure for the poachers at this time of year and the salmon are the bait, while Ivan Swaile and his men are the invisible net in which the poachers entangle themselves.

At spawning time Ivan and his men sometimes find eggs left on the bank, which means that someone has been taking the fish.

'If they get away with it once, the poachers will come back to the same place at the same time the next year,' Ivan said. 'But what they don't know is that next time we shall be waiting for them.'

Such desperate deeds at dead of night seem more appropriate to tales of smugglers and excise men in the old days, but for Ivan Swaile they are nothing out of the ordinary. He drove me to the scene of a recent incident which had all the ingredients of a good thriller.

'It started one December day with a telephone call from the local farmer,' Ivan said. 'The farmer was complaining that we had been parking our short-wheeled Land Rover in his field and making a hell of a mess of his land. "If I could have caught your men, I'd have given them a right rollicking," he said. I told him I'd look into it,' Ivan said. 'The interesting thing about that telephone call was that we don't use Land Rovers, but I knew of a gang of poachers from Bishop Auckland who did.'

The police in Bishop Auckland were alerted and, sure enough, a few nights later, Ivan was woken in the middle of the night by a telephone call from the police.

'Mr B. is heading west,' they said.

Ivan called up his men and they drove to the farm where the Land Rover had been seen. They left their van well out of sight over a hill and walked back to the river where they could see torchlight glinting through the trees from the river bank. They waited. ('There's a lot of waiting involved in catching poachers,' Ivan said.) Eventually they heard the men coming back across the field from the river.

'I was behind a wall with three lads,' Ivan said. 'When the poachers reached their Land Rover, we rushed them. They put up a tremendous fight, but we got one of them halfway across that field over there and we got the fish and we got the Land Rover. The other men got away, but they'd have had a long walk home: it must be forty miles to Bishop Auckland from here.' Ivan smiled. . . . One more set of intruders put to flight.

'The modern poacher is not a countryman,' Ivan commented. 'He has no feeling for the countryside, no respect for the river.'

Ivan himself feels a personal involvement in his river. Someone told him once that the River Wye in Herefordshire was an outstanding river, so he went and had a look at it.

'It was just lying there,' he said, 'doing nothing. Still and dead.' Ivan's river bounces over its grey stones with reckless glee. 'Every burn and beck that comes tumbling down from the hills ends up in my river,' he said with quiet pride . . . 'Every one of them.'

> *What have they,*
> *The bookish townsmen in their dry retreats,*
> *Known of December dawns, before the sun*
> *Reddened the east, and the fields were wet and grey?*
>
> *When have they gone, another day begun*
> *By tracks into a quagmire trodden,*
> *With sacks about their shoulders and the damp*
> *Soaking until their very souls were sodden,*
> *To help a sick beast, by a flickering lamp,*
> *With rough words and kind hands?*

(Vita Sackville-West, *The Land*)

When you live in the country, 'birth and death are both natural things', as Venning Davey had said. But if a farmer thinks he can save one of his animals, he will go to endless trouble to do so, and that is partly, but not wholly, because of the money involved. Farmers display a strange mixture of sentiment and practicality: Stan Hayles, for instance, told me how he had saved an injured lamb with some makeshift doctoring. Veterinary surgeons cost money and only get called in when a farmer is desperate, or in danger of losing a really valuable animal.

He explained that, one December, he discovered that one of his lambs had broken its leg.

'It had been kicked by a horse,' he said. 'When I found it, the leg was all waving about and I could feel that it was broken in three places. It was an awful mess and I didn't know what I was going to do with it. Anyway I got some bandage and I put that on first. I had to sort of shape the leg with that; and then I found two little bits of plastic stick with flat sides to them that I'd been keeping for to go inside of a motor . . . and I used them as splints, and then I put a plastic bag over the whole lot to keep it dry.

'Within two days that lamb was putting its foot down on the ground. I thought to myself that broken bones usually take about six weeks to heal up, so I left it about that long and when I took the bandage off, the leg was as good as new. I was quite proud of myself.'

'He doesn't like to be beaten, you know,' his wife said, smiling. 'He'll find some way round a problem if he can. He was as pleased as Punch when he saved that lamb.'

December is John Richardson's busiest month of the year. He keeps 10,000 turkeys on his farm in Surrey and from 1st December until Christmas Day he works a sixteen-hour day to prepare and hand-pluck the birds destined for the Christmas market.

Because it takes twenty weeks for a turkey to reach the required weight and maturity, John Richardson gets his day-old chicks from the turkey hatcheries in July . . . but those chicks have to be ordered the previous September.

'What I want to know is: are you going to invite your Granny to Christmas dinner, not this year, but next year?' John Richardson said.

After thirty years in the business, John Richardson probably knows more about how the average British family is going to spend its Christmas than they know themselves.

'It all depends what day of the week Christmas falls on,' he said.

Apparently the demand for the biggest birds comes when Christmas falls on a Friday, because that means that most people will not be able to buy fresh meat for four days.

Turkeys originated in Central and North America where they were hunted by the Red Indians, who used their feathers to decorate their head-dresses. The first turkeys arrived in England in the sixteenth century and were proclaimed by King James I as 'King of birds – bird of kings'. Turkeys bred in Norfolk during the seventeenth and eighteenth centuries were driven to London on foot: they started their journey in August wearing little leather boots to protect their feet, and arrived, stringily, in November.

John Richardson's turkeys are white feathered and broad breasted. Looking into one of his open-sided barns where the birds are kept, you see a winter landscape of white feathers, sprouting thin, pink necks and small, watchful heads. There is a constant babble of gentle musical sound.

'That's crowd noise,' John said. 'They're talking to one another.'

John's faith in his turkeys has been rewarded. Since he set up in business the demand for turkeys has risen steadily by one million birds a year and there seems no reason why it should not go on rising as turkey meat is fashionably high in protein and low in cholesterol. It all sounds like good tidings of great joy. The two-ounce turkey poults arrive in their cardboard boxes in July and go into heated brooder houses where they 'positively explode', – as John Richardson put it – they put on weight so fast. The poults convert every two pounds of food they eat into one pound of turkey.

'They put everything they've got into growth for eighteen weeks,' John said, 'and then they spend the last two weeks maturing.'

But if all the stags and all the hen turkeys for the Christmas market mature simultaneously, what about the people who want a small or medium-sized turkey for their dinner? Easy. A small or medium-sized turkey, it turns out, is not a forty-pounder brought to an untimely end, but a different strain of turkey which has been bred to mature at a different weight. It is because different strains of turkey mature at different weights that John Richardson needs second sight when he is ordering his day-old chicks.

John Richardson is a great champion of the turkey, but surely the tidings cannot all be joyful?

'I suppose you could say they're stupid,' he said. 'You can have a poult sitting on two inches of food and dying of starvation because it hasn't the sense to eat it.'

Yes, I'd say that was depressing.

'Turkeys are colour conscious, you see,' John Richardson explained. 'We have to have contrasting colours for the feeders and drinkers to keep them interested.'

What colours do turkeys like best?

'No, no. What I mean is that the wood flakes on the floor and the food we're giving them to eat are roughly the same colour, so we make sure that the feeders and drinkers are brightly coloured so they will stand out. What I mean is that turkeys are contrast conscious.'

It is astonishing to think that the turkeys that walked from Norfolk to London could possibly have arrived alive, since turkeys have no sense whatever of self-preservation. When the poults first arrive they are kept under the warmth of the brooders by a circular wooden barrier. It has to be circular because if it was square the poults would get into the corners and suffocate. And when an owl got into one of his barns one night, John found forty turkeys dead the next morning: they had piled on top of one another in their panic and smothered themselves.

'They are suicidal little beggars,' John Richardson said.

John is a happy and energetic man. He keeps his birds from thoughts of self-destruction and prides himself on supplying his customers with what they want. And there his responsibilities end – or they should do. Unfortunately, not every turkey falls into safe hands. One Christmas a young newly-married couple ordered a 36-pound turkey from him. They had decided to celebrate their first Christmas in style and had invited both sets of parents and assorted aunts and uncles to dinner. They put the turkey into the oven on Christmas Eve, got up the next morning and went to church. When they came home they were surprised to find the turkey still in the oven. They had forgotten all about it and it was burnt black. They rang up John Richardson and told him what had happened.

'We've chipped off the outside and it doesn't look too bad inside, but what can we do?' they asked him.

By an incredible stroke of luck he happened to have one ten-pounder left, so he sold them that to cook and put on the table for show while they chipped away at the original turkey in the privacy of the kitchen.

John put his hands over his face.

'When some of my customers talk about how they are going to cook my turkeys, they terrify me.'

When the Earls Court Exhibition Centre opens its doors in December for the annual Royal Smithfield Show, it attracts farmers from all over the British Isles. Visitors to the Show are confronted first of all by the newest examples of farm machinery, gleaming slurry guzzlers, spray applicators, potato planters, rotary tillers, dirt blasters, big bale hoppers and ever bigger and more powerful tractors with tyres that reach as high as your hat. The farmers wander between the monsters, watching the videos which come from all directions showing the machines in action, all filmed in idyllic scenery and beautiful weather. The farmers take it all in and remain carefully non-committal, stopping only briefly as they move around to greet long-lost friends with the same lack of fuss: 'Hello John. How are you?' A quick handshake and they pass on.

Upstairs there are more machines and the sheep and the pigs – the sheep looked hot under the lights. One of them, brought out of its pen to compete in the ring, fell over and covered its coat with straw.

'Now look what you've done!' said its exasperated owner, lifting it back onto its feet and picking straw out of its coat as fast as he could.

Over in the pig ring, tradition holds fast. Only in the pig ring do the officials still wear dark suits and bowler hats, bringing a touch of dignity to the otherwise chaotic proceedings. In a class for Large White pigs there were pigs dashing in all directions.

'Yes, they're difficult animals to control,' said Lionel Organ, a pig breeder from Cheltenham.

The handlers were trying hard to keep their exuberant charges still long enough for the judges to have a look at them, coaxing them to stand still with bowls of food and apples, and carrying two boards to push into their faces when they were heading in the wrong direction.

'It's the only way you can control the little blighters,' Lionel Organ said. 'If they want to go left, right, straight on or into reverse, they will. The only way is to shove something in their faces and hope they will think it's a wall.'

Just at that moment one pig galloped across the ring, collided head-on with the netting and ended up in a sitting position looking surprised. The judge finally awarded the first prize to Lionel Organ's pig. Royal Catalina she was called. Lionel Organ has 150 breeding sows on his farm, the Southam Herd of Pedigree Large Whites..

'It's my hobby and my life,' he said. 'I just love the damn' things. I love them for their mischievous ways. Intelligent? They're over-intelligent. They try to outwit us and we are supposed to be the most intelligent of all the animals, aren't we? I had an old chap work for me once who used to say that every time he saw a pig he wanted to hit it. I asked him why that was and he said "Because it's either coming back from mischief or going to it." And that's very true. If you hit every pig you saw, you wouldn't be far out, but of course we never hit our pigs. They live a life of luxury and eat as much as they want.'

Lionel Organ's pigs all have curly tails because with unrestricted feeding there is no danger of tail-biting. Lionel Organ has spent the last twenty years breeding pigs that can eat to their hearts' content without getting fat.

'What would have been a good pig twenty years ago would be a terrible pig now,' he said. His pigs are long and lean, but all the meat is at the rear end where the best meat comes from, which, he told me, is 'the opposite to nature'.

'A wild boar would have had a big front and shoulders and not too much at the back. We have completely turned nature around.'

Lionel said that he gave his pigs 'a lovely life'.

'We build up a lot of trust between ourselves and the pigs,' he said. 'So people say to me, if that's true, how can you kill them? The answer is that you have to be prepared up here,' he said, tapping his head, 'although I'm lucky in that respect because a lot of my pigs don't have to be killed. They go for breeding.

'But I don't care what these vegetarian freaks say, I'm a meat eater myself and I think it would be a sad look-out if they had their way and there were no animals in the countryside. I am pretty sure that the balance of nature was designed and made to give us animals to eat. All I care about is that the animals should have happy lives and when the time comes, that their end should be quick and painless.'

The judge had gone for lunch and the last of the pigs from the ring were being guided back to their pens. Men in white coats were racing between the stands; somewhere a pig was on the loose. Lionel Organ's pigs were asleep, exhausted after all that exercise, but the pig in the next pen stuck his snout into the wire mesh and barked, a definite 'ruff, ruff' sound.

'Pigs bark when they're happy,' Lionel Organ said, smiling down at them. 'And of course they squeal. We have to tattoo our number on their ears and that can be painful for everyone con-cerned. For a start pigs don't like being held and you really do have to hold them tight for that; so your face is right next to theirs, and if they squeal on a certain wavelength, it really makes your ears sing. I don't blame them, though. I'd squeal if somebody tattooed my ear, wouldn't you?'

The difficulty about the Smithfield Show is that so much happens at the same time. Downstairs in the Cattle Ring it was time for

Class 44A: Cross-bred Heifers, not exceeding fifteen months old, sired by bulls of European Origin. Andy Frazier would be exhibiting his heifer. I had visited him near Kidderminster three weeks before to find out how he prepared a beast for the show, and had found him in a cattle shed, comb in hand, working on the heifer's coat. The heifer was called the Lady in Red.

'Thinking of names for them is a problem,' Andy said. He had named her after the song. 'It means a lot to me, that song,' he explained.

The Lady was not shaping up in the way he had hoped. Andy, a slim young man, full of nervous energy, stood and watched her as she dashed from one side of the shed to the other.

'She's not bad, but she's still a little bit on the small side, and she's far too frisky at the moment. I haven't even been able to get a halter on her yet,' he said. 'Every time I try she throws herself on the floor in a tantrum.'

Entries for the Smithfield Show have to be in by the first week in September, which means taking a bit of a gamble with a young animal who might or might not be ready when the time comes. Cattle showmen like Andy Frazier are always on the look-out for a likely beast. Andy has the shape he is looking for imprinted on his mind.

'When you first see them, they might be bedraggled and covered in mud, but you have to be able to undress them in your mind's eye,' he said. 'With cross-bred beef cattle, it's all about meat in the right places.'

The Lady was a good shape, squarish and well balanced, with back and belly running parallel. A real winner has to have that indefinable star quality though, – 'that bit of flash' as Andy put it, just as the Lady in Red flashed past him again.

Preparing an animal for Smithfield can take anything up to twelve weeks. This includes feeding them carefully, working on the coat (cattle shampoo costs £10 a gallon) and walking them for one and a half miles a day behind a tractor, to keep the flesh firm and to teach them to walk quietly. The Lady in Red was due to go out walking as soon as the rain eased off, Andy explained, giving her a reproachful look as she tangoed round a corner.

Andy Frazier has been showing at Smithfield since 1979. The first time he went there he did not know anything about the sort of last-minute preparation that goes on behind the show ring.

'I watched everyone else and saw all these people with their blowers (hair dryers) and clippers and all that and I asked one or two people what I should do,' he said. 'They are the finest stockmen in the world there, you know, the best.'

Andy's show box is now full of 'goodies' – shampoo, paint for the hooves, clippers and combs, blower and talcum powder. 'You put talcum powder on any white bits of your animal to brighten them up,' said Andy. 'The only trouble is that if you are waiting to go into the ring and your animal bumps into a black one, all the talcum powder flies up and lands on the black one, and you can imagine what the man leading the black one thinks about that.' He laughed.

As far as he can remember, the first time he showed an animal at Smithfield it was not even clipped, but now Andy is an expert with the clippers. An expert job with the clippers means that it is impossible to tell where the animal ends and the hair begins.

'If you get a beast with a good coat, a coat like a teddy bear, you can do a lot with it. You can fool a lot of people, you know. They say you can never fool a good judge,' Andy said, 'but you bloody well can. I've seen it done. Some animals that win prizes – if you threw a bucket of water over them, there wouldn't be a lot left. It's like seeing Miss World without her make-up, isn't it?'

When the cattle have been washed, clipped and combed, the final touch for the show is to back-comb the end of the tail.

'If you look at an animal from behind, you can see that where the body finishes, there's just a pair of legs and an empty space,' Andy said. 'But when the tail has been back-combed into a ball, you see, it fills the gap.'

I saw, but I still find it difficult to take a beast seriously with a fluffy pom-pom dangling from the end of its tail.

The seats all round the Cattle Ring at Smithfield were packed with spectators and there was Andy Frazier, leading the Lady in Red round the ring on a dazzling white rope halter and she was walking with her head in the air and as quiet as could be – 'walking proud' was how Andy had described it. The judge in the centre of the ring was watching all the animals carefully. Andy had told me that his first goal was to get among those asked to line up for a closer inspection by the judge.

'You have to stay in there and convince the judge you mean business,' he said. 'We all know a lot about cattle but, in the end, it comes down to that one man's decision, so I have to convince him that I have the winning animal and I never give up until the prize cards have been handed out.'

The Judge picked out some of the cattle and sent the others away out of the ring. The Lady in Red was still there: I felt like cheering. The commentator was pointing out that the classes this year were 'maintaining the usual high standard expected of competitors at Smithfield', as he was sure we would all agree. The Lady in Red was standing beautifully – 'with a leg in each corner' as her owner would have put it. Some of the other leaders were having difficulty getting their animals to stand square. One leader pushed his beast's legs with a stick to get it to move its foot, but when it did move, it stood on his toe. The man's face turned bright pink above his white coat and his lips formed a silent 'ooh' of anguish.

The judge had a close look at all the cattle as they stood in line.

'I always make stacks of noise,' Andy had told me. 'As the judge comes to the beast next to mine, I'll cough or sneeze or do anything I can to catch his attention and the minute I catch his eye, I throw my eye onto my animal and his eye will follow mine. If I'm not picked out to be in the "front row", I will keep on catching his eye and try to make him feel guilty, make him feel that he's making a mistake. I've known judges change their minds at the very last minute.'

The judge was making his decision and getting the animals into their final order.

'To finish in the final line-up is an honour in itself,' said the commentator.

In the end, the Lady in Red was awarded Fifth Prize on the day when she was eight months and seventeen days old, and weighed 357 kilograms, which, considering all the problems Andy Frazier had been having with her, was a considerable achievement for both of them.

I found Andy in the cattle-lines behind the show-ring a little later. He was smiling broadly, savouring his triumph.

'She did well, didn't she?' he said. 'It was hard work . . . very hard work, but it was worth it.'

The Lady was relaxing and chewing her cud under the tasteful brown winner's card which was hanging up over her head. She had been well named. As it says in the song: 'Lady in red . . . you were amazing.'

And each man knows the life that fits him best,
The shape it makes his soul, the tune, the tone,
And after ranging on a tentative flight
Stoops like a merlin to the constant lure.
The country habit has me by the heart.

(Vita Sackville-West, *The Land*)